Wish
Kisses
from
Heaven

About The Author

Rev. Dr. Derry James-Tannariello is Board Certified with the Association of Professional Chaplains, and carries a BA in Religion; BS in Personal Ministries and Psychology; MA in Christian Psychology; Master of Divinity; and Doctor of Ministry specializing in Christian Counseling. She has also been awarded VIP Woman of the Year by the National Association of Professional Women.

Derry founded Chaplain Services at Sierra Nevada Memorial Hospital in California. Hospitals, churches, educational institutions and other community organizations solicit her expertise in training others to minister to the sick and terminally ill, and for help dealing with loss and grief.

Derry is a retired healthcare chaplain, author, and sought-after speaker known for her compassionate heart, humor and life-changing inspirational stories of faith and wisdom. She is an internationally recognized seminar and workshop presenter and an interdenominational guest speaker and lecturer on topics of "How to Have an Effective Prayer Life," "Personal Transformation," "Relational God," "Spirituality and Health" and many more spiritually uplifting topics.

Derry also speaks and presents seminars on "Spiritual Support in Palliative Care," "Bereavement and Grief," "End of Life," "Ministering to Our Dying Loved Ones," "Effective Hospital Visitation" and other topics in hospital ministry.

Derry resides part-time in New Hampshire and part-time in Florida with her husband, where she assumes pastoral responsibilities, offers spiritual guidance, chaplain support, and enjoys teaching classes based upon her training and experience.

Derry has authored a number of other books, shown and described at the end of this book. To learn more about her, her other books, or to have her as a speaker for your event, workshop or organization, visit her website:

FreedomInSurrender.net

With Kisses from Heaven

Stories of Adventures in Faith

Mercy and truth have met together;
*Righteousness and peace have **kissed**.*

—

Psalm 85:10

Freedom in Surrender Publishing
Amherst, New Hampshire

Derry James-Tannariello, DMin BCC

Published by Freedom in Surrender Publishing.

For book signings, bulk purchases and inquiries, contact the author at her website: FreedomInSurrender.net.

To order *With Kisses From Heaven* or any other titles by this author, visit: FreedomInSurrender.net.

Publisher's Cataloging-in-Publication Data
James-Tannariello, Derry
    with kisses from heaven : stories of adventures in faith / by
    Derry James-Tannariello, DMin BCC.—1st ed.
        p. cm.
    ISBN-13: 978-0-9980152-7-9
    ISBN-10: 0-9980152-7-X
    1. Prayer. 2. Pastoral Theology. 3. Worship. 4. God-Christianity.
    5. Jesus Christ. 6. Holy Spirit. I. James-Tannariello, Derry.
    II. Title.

Library of Congress Control Number: 2020945922

Some of the anecdotal illustrations in this book are true to life and are included with the permission of the persons involved. All other illustrations are composites of real situations, and any resemblance to people living or dead is coincidental.

Printed in the United States of America

Dedication

I dedicate this book and its companion book *With Gladness Every Day* to my Father, my Lord Jesus—my dearest friend, and my Counselor Holy Spirit, Who is the real Author and Finisher of these books.

Also to my beloved grandchildren: Seth, Samuel, Simon, Benjamin, Talitha and Noah; my spiritual grandchildren Mathew and Dayver; and to all my husband's grandchildren he so graciously shares with me—all 22 of them!

I pray our grandchildren will grow up loving and trusting our precious Savior with a deep-rooted commitment to live for and obey God with all their hearts, minds and souls. May these stories of God's love and provision become a legacy for their life of service to Him.

I also dedicate these books to my sons who walked through some of these same heartaches, challenges and miraculous blessings with me. May you be reminded of how God was present and know He will always be there for you. At this time we are far from each other but I pray we will all gather in the courts of heaven with our loving Savior.

I love you,
Mom.

The Butterfly

As love falls down from the sky,
It lands on the wings of a butterfly.
The butterfly sings its songs and rhymes,
And flies through the air, no concept of time.
It is the messenger of patience and change,
From flower to flower, it's odd and it's strange.
The butterfly can transform its world,
And give way to new beginnings, unfurled.
It is the keeper of transformation,
And flies on faith and imagination.
The butterfly has no fear of change,
It bravely escapes its homemade cage.
To change, it knows is necessary,
For all the burdens we need not carry.
The butterfly soars, and merrily sings,
For, without change, it could never grow wings.

—Heather Reneé Adamkiewicz

Contents

Preface

It has been about 45 years since God first spoke to me about writing the companion book to this book, *With Gladness Every Day*. For the full story and background, I hope you will get a copy of *With Gladness Every Day* and read the Preface.

With Kisses From Heaven came about because of the abundance of stories I have accumulated highlighting God's magnificent love and the countless ways He expresses it. There were more stories than could fit in *With Gladness*. God was surprising us with so much love—a little here and a little there—that I coined the phrase, that's another "kiss from heaven." When a second book was needed it seemed the perfect title; *With Kisses From Heaven*. Now there are more stories than can fit into *With Kisses* so the next book coming out will be *With Love Overflowing*. Book three is soon to follow.

When I have been at a point of giving up writing, I remember the cards of encouragement given to me when I attended a Book Expo many years ago. One said, "God is with you! Expect a miracle." The picture on it was of a baby duck standing up sticking the tip of its little webbed toes in the water. The other was a picture of a little mouse about to grab the cheese from a mousetrap. It said, "Only go through the doors God opens." I sensed God prompting—encouraging me that He would speak through me and help me accomplish this task. I have carried these cards ever since. They have been a reminder that God gave me the title *With Gladness Every Day* because He had a book in mind.

Over these past 45 years God has been developing the content through His interventions in my life and in the lives of those I love, by my life experiences, spiritual growth, answered prayers and His saving grace and incomprehensible love. The last few years I have written an occasional story and filed it away. Now He is directing me to put these stories together to bring hope to a troubled world.

With Kisses From Heaven

I have been completing this manuscript and the companion books *With Gladness Every Day* and *With Love Overflowing* during the 2020 pandemic. Terrorism abounds. Our world is mired in fear and despair. God has chosen the writing of these books for such a time as this. This is a time in history when people want to know God is real. He cares about this world and He delights to answer prayer and prove He is relational.

In two of my previous books, *Praying in the "Yes" of God* and *Growing in the "Yes" of God,* many who have stood by me and contributed to the success of these books are mentioned by name in my acknowledgements. I would like to thank some of them again here: Ann Cuddy-Sullivan for her amazing job developing and keeping current my website, offering suggestions, and turning my manuscripts into e-books for me. Ray Fusci who is a gifted editor and designer has blessed me with his many talents and always has valuable suggestions we implement. It has been his confidence in me, and his desire to get these stories in print that has helped keep me motivated. His sacrificial labor and professional knowledge has produced books I am proud to put my name on. I thank God for His gift to me in Ray and trust that God will reward him for all he has done to help share Jesus with the world through these books. A big thank-you to his wife Cathy, my dear friend, who has patiently shared Ray's time to get these books completed.

I also want to thank the many new friends I have met in my travels and seminar presenting, who have fanned the flame within me and kept me motivated by requesting that I write a book.

Last but not least I thank my beloved husband who not only lived some of these stories with me but carved out time to read the manuscripts and has offered valuable insights that contributed greatly to their content. Thank you to all of you with sincere love and deepest appreciation

Birthed from 45 years of living life and experiencing God, I lovingly present to you *With Kisses From Heaven.*

Introduction

Frequently after I have spoken at a seminar or conference, I have been asked if I have written a book containing my stories. I am finally doing just that. Presently I have divided some of my stories into two books. *With Gladness Every Day* is divided into "Answers to Prayer" and "Life Experiences." *With Kisses From Heaven* is divided into "God's Intervention" and "Scripture Lessons." *With Love Overflowing* validates Jesus as a personal friend. All stories illustrate God's extravagant, incomprehensible, unconditional love and ways.

Our wonderful, loving Father delights in making Himself known to His children. One way He communicates with us is by answering our prayers. God loves to commune and be in a relationship with us. The desire of my heart is to help show that Jesus is alive today!!! He is a caring and loving God Who longs for a relationship with each of us. He hears and answers our prayers. If you are having difficulty developing a personal relationship with Him, or believing He answers prayer, I recommend reading His #1 best seller, *The Bible*. I would also refer you to my books *Praying in the "Yes" of God* and *Growing in the "Yes" of God,* which I pray will help you implement God's word.

Throughout the books I have written you will read "God said" or "I heard" or some other similar expression. When I say that, it doesn't mean I heard an audible voice (although I have at times). I am referring to that inner voice He speaks quietly to your mind or heart; sometimes it is a 'knowing' or a 'sense of His presence.' Sometimes God speaks through friends but He lets you know in your heart it is from Him, sometimes through what you read in Scripture or inspirational books, through music, nature, or providential workings. God has many ways of "speaking" to us and making sure we hear Him. In this book, by sharing how involved He is in every aspect of our lives. I hope He will speak to you and it will 'whet your appetite' for more of Him.

The first section includes Scripture lessons derived from life experiences. The Holy Spirit gives spiritual insights that work transformation in our life and minister to our heart.

The second section of this book is about God's interventions—the magnificence of His love and the multitude of ways He expresses it to us. Look for a word of thanksgiving or praise. Many times we fail to recognize His presence in our life. If we don't notice His involvement, then we probably don't thank Him. So often we "ask" God but forget to express our appreciation.

Life happens; the challenges and the joys. Do we just make it through each day or do we stop a minute to reflect? What happened today? How did I see God in this? What can I learn from today's experience? Is there anything I need to change? Anything I need to take care of? Anyone I need to address? Every day is a new day of life and opportunities. We can make it by barely hanging on or we can learn, grow, love, share and make a difference for good. We can shape our own world or let the world shape us. We can make a decision to take time to let the Lord work His life into ours.

I hope these encounters resonate with you and cause you to wonder about your own experiences with God and what lessons were in them for you. I pray that my sharing has primed the pump and causes you to think back and reflect.

My purpose for these books is a reminder to myself and, I hope, to impress upon your heart, that our God is a personal, caring God Who loves you extravagantly and is aware of everything that concerns you. He is there for you, even in silence. If we open our hearts and minds, we will see and experience the outpouring of His love; a love that will kindle a desire to be more like Him.

Kisses From Heaven

Are you aware of the kisses you get from heaven? Are you cognizant of those daily blessings—small and large? Do you take a minute to acknowledge God and thank Him when they arrive?

The definition of kisses is: touch with the lips as a sign of love; lightly and gently touch; to come into contact usually to express love or affection. Similarly there are air kisses and soul kisses used to express affection.

So what in the world do I mean "With Kisses from Heaven?" To me, a "kiss" from heaven is that unexpected act of love, that surprise gentle touch of love, that puts a smile on your face and maybe causes you to say "ahhh" or "oh wow" or thank You Lord, so much! It is something God does for you beyond what you have asked, or gives you without you asking, that catches you off guard and makes you feel loved.

A "kiss from heaven" is something that adds an unexpected joy or delight to your day. It can be as simple as a butterfly landing on your arm, a bird perched on a branch close to where you are sitting, singing you a song, or any surprise interlude with nature. There are many "kisses" God sends to us in nature.

Kisses are divine interventions that can come in many different ways. It could come as a special gift, a surprise call or card in the mail of affirmation or encouragement, an answer to a cry for help, deliverance from a dangerous situation, or an awareness or insight of something God wants us to know or understand—a different perspective, an enlightenment. However it comes, it is special and is imparted by God Who lovingly assures us in James 1:17 NIV, *Every good and perfect gift is from above, coming down from the Father ...* and in Isaiah 65:24 NIV God reminds us *Before they call I will answer; while they are still speaking I will hear.*

With Kisses From Heaven

In Psalm 36:10, because David knew God, he requested, *Oh, continue Your lovingkindness to those who know You, And Your righteousness to the upright in heart.* Loving kindness! Now that's a great way of expressing a "kiss from heaven!"

I can only imagine God smiling and enjoying our reaction when He surprises us. May your heart thrill as you become more and more aware of God's daily provision, watchful care and unexpected blessings of love He generously bestows upon you.

The following stories are about surprises that God sends in various ways—*With Kisses from Heaven.* May they help you become aware of all the ways God shows you His incomprehensible, irresistible love and sends you His Kisses.

 Butterfly Kiss:

"How does one become a butterfly?" she asked. "You must want to fly so much that you are willing to give up being a caterpillar."

—Trina Paulus

Section I: Scripture Lessons

Daily Jesus went to His Father for instruction. When Jesus returned to heaven, God sent us the gift of the Holy Spirit for empowerment, enlightenment, understanding and daily direction. The Holy Spirit is promised in John 14:26, *But the Helper, the Holy Spirit, whom the Father will send in My name, He will teach you all things, and bring to your remembrance all things that I said to you.*

The Holy Spirit will help us learn, give us spiritual insights and prepare us to effectively fulfill God's plans to serve others and be about heaven's business. As scripture lessons are illuminated through our life experiences, they will work a transformation in us to better reflect Christ's character and minister more effectively on His behalf.

... A man can receive nothing unless it has been given to him from heaven.—John 3:27.

The LORD will fight for you, and you shall hold your peace.
    —Exodus 14:14.

God brings no man into the conflicts of life to desert him. Every man has a friend in heaven whose resources are unlimited; and on Him he may call at any hour and find sympathy and assistance.

    —Robert A. Morris

casting all your care upon Him, for He cares for you.—1 Peter 5:7.

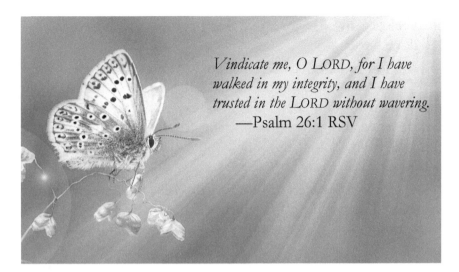

Vindicate me, O LORD, for I have walked in my integrity, and I have trusted in the LORD without wavering.
—Psalm 26:1 RSV

Accused

As a child, so impressionable, many things form us and teach us about life. One lesson we learn over and over is whether adults are trustworthy or if we need to be cautious around them.

Have you ever been unjustly accused of taking something? I have—twice. What a horrible feeling of helplessness captured me. Both times there was no way of proving my innocence. I had to depend completely on Jesus to vindicate me.

The first time I was only 12 years old. An older couple had moved in with us while they were relocating. The man helped my dad at the service station we owned. The woman was home with us. She loved to cook and wow could she cook up some great meals. She was from New Orleans and loved to do Cajun cooking. Some of the meals she served were like nothing I had ever had. The fragrance alone had you watching the clock yearning for supper.

She kept to herself a lot, but I liked her ... until just before they left. One afternoon I heard my mother calling, "Derry Lee! Where are you?" I knew something was wrong. Mother never called me "Derry Lee" unless I was in **big** trouble. I reluctantly answered. I couldn't come up with anything I had done wrong.

Mother had decided to make a nice goodbye meal for our guests. When Mom set a special table, it was beautiful. She had a talent for design and was also very crafty. She had plans for the table tonight and was trying to get everything ready. She had been looking for her good tablecloth and couldn't find it.

I quickly arrived at Mom's side. Before I could speak, she did. "Where is my good tablecloth?"

With a quizzical look, I stammered, "How would I know?"

"Millie told me she saw you digging through the cupboard and take something folded out and run away."

"What? That wasn't me. Maybe it was my sister."

"Millie saw you. I can't believe that you're lying to me. I have always trusted you. We're not going to start stealing or lying in this house young lady. Come with me."

Far be it from me to tell you what happened when mother took me to the other room. But I will tell you I begged her to reconsider. I told her again it wasn't me and that I wouldn't lie to her. Mother was very upset and there was no talking her out of it. In her mind I deserved to be punished, and punished I was. I was also forbidden, at the risk of further punishment, to say anything to Millie regarding this. Needless to say my heart wasn't the only thing that hurt that night. I went to bed in tears. I asked Jesus to please show my mother that I didn't do it.

Two days later, my mother sat down on the sofa and called me to her side. "Derry, I need to talk to you. I have done something very wrong, but I'm not sorry. While Millie was in town yesterday with her husband, I did something I feel very guilty about. I went through her suitcase. But I'm glad I did. In her suitcase I found the tablecloth that you were accused of taking. I took it out of her suitcase and returned it to its place in the cupboard.

Ever since I punished you I have not had peace. You don't lie to me and I couldn't imagine why you would need or want a tablecloth and why you would lie about taking it if you had wanted to use it. I am so sorry, Honey. What a terrible thing that woman did to blame you and watch me punish you. I am so glad they are gone. Please forgive me for not believing you and for jumping to conclusions."

In my distress I cried to the LORD, *And He heard me.*—Psalm 120:1.

Even though I was just a child, I knew God had intervened for me and had answered my prayer. I didn't want my mother to think she couldn't trust my word, but the devil wanted to destroy my credibility. God vindicated me and protected my reputation.

The second time was just as traumatic, but I was much older. I had recently moved in among new friends. None of us knew each other well. One day, one of the other boarders came up to me and in a very accusing voice demanded, "What did you do with my necklace?"

"I don't know anything about your necklace," I replied

"You took it. You're the only one here that could have taken it."

"I don't even wear jewelry," I said.

"You took my necklace and I want it back."

There was no convincing any different. I was guilty in their eyes and nothing I said could convince them otherwise.

The subject came up over and over. One day with a finger right in my face I was yelled at, accused and threatened that I had better return it before the day was over. I had nothing to produce.

I was heartbroken. I love Jesus and wanted to express His love and character to these strangers I had moved in with.

Now, I was shunned, distrusted and under suspicion and surveillance.

Months went by and the accusations increased. In fact, anytime anything was misplaced I was accused of taking it. Another attack came. I broke down and sobbed. I asked if they really believed that I would destroy my testimony and endure all this verbal abuse over a necklace. They yelled and screamed and then ignored me.

Very broken and heartsick I closed myself in my room and sobbed. Crying out to Jesus, which I had already done regarding this trial a number of times, I told the Lord I couldn't deal with this any longer. I implored God to clear my name, to vindicate me. He reminded me of His promise in Psalm 116:1-2, *I love the LORD, because He has heard my voice and my supplications. Because He has inclined His ear to me, Therefore I will call* upon Him *as long as I live.*

A few weeks later we were all getting ready to leave the house when what did I see draped around the neck of my "friend" but the "stolen" necklace. I stood there stunned. "Do you mean to tell me the necklace was found and I wasn't even told, confronted, or apologized to?"

I was acknowledged with a laugh. "Oh, I found it in the zipper pocket of my suitcase. Sorry."

A flippant, arrogant "sorry" was all I got. It was difficult for me to believe that someone could be so despicable and cowardly that they couldn't 'fess up and apologize.

For me ... even though I was hurt, I was grateful the Lord had cleared my name. Through all the judgments I had endured, I knew God knew the truth and even though things weren't going well in relationships around me, all was well with the Lord and this girl!

When we go through heartache and trials, sometimes the only way we have the courage to carry on is to know God is on our side and He will clear things up.

*The L*ORD *judges the peoples; judge me, O L*ORD, *according to my right-eousness and according to the integrity that is in me.*—Psalm 7:8 RSV.

The scripture lesson here for me is to remember that God is our Judge and Advocate and He will vindicate us. His word is true. His timing is His own. If we are misunderstood or wrongfully accused or judged, eventually God will vindicate us. In the meantime, we must strengthen our faith, bless our accusers and hold onto Him. May God bless you with peace.

Scripture Kiss brought:
> Vindication.

Therefore do not worry about tomorrow, for tomorrow will worry about its own things. Sufficient for the day is its own trouble.—Matthew 6:34.

 Butterfly Kiss:
> We delight in the beauty of the butterfly, but rarely admit the changes it has gone through to achieve that beauty.
> — Maya Angelou

With Kisses From Heaven

Greet one another with a kiss of love. Peace to you all who are in Christ Jesus. Amen.—1 Peter 5:14.

> Holding on to anger, resentment and hurt only gives you tense muscles, a headache and a sore jaw from clenching your teeth. Forgiveness gives you back the laughter and the lightness in your life.
>
> —Joan Lunden

 Butterfly Kiss:
Just like the butterfly, I too will awaken in my own time.
—Deborah Chaskin

to speak evil of no one, to avoid quarreling, to be gentle, and to show perfect courtesy toward all men.
—Titus 3:2 RSV.

Anger In The Prayer Closet

I look forward to and thoroughly enjoy the days I can wake up and go over to the piano, play a few praise songs to the Lord and then grab my Bible and hide out with God.

For my birthday one year I asked God what text He wanted me to make my focus for growth in the coming year. I was thrilled with His answer, because it was the longing of my heart. This would be a great scripture promise to memorize and bring before Him for fulfillment in my life daily. My birthday text was Ephesians 5:1-2, *Therefore be imitators of God as dear children. And walk in love, as Christ also has loved us and given Himself for us, an offering and a sacrifice to God for a sweet-smelling aroma.*

I realize I fall so short, but the desire of my heart is to reflect Christ and leave behind a sweet smelling aroma of His presence. I become a "new creation" when I am able to spend quality time with Him. Jeremiah 30:19 ESV says, *Out of them shall come songs of thanksgiving, and the voices of those who celebrate...* That's how I feel—like celebrating.

One morning as I was basking in my "prayer closet" praising God with all my heart, sensing the presence of the

Holy Spirit, my husband interrupted me. Now I love my husband, but this interruption was over something very insignificant that could have waited all day if necessary, but only a few more minutes would have been nice, in my thinking.

Here I am praising God and now mystified and annoyed at my husband's intrusion. I laugh as I write this. What an anomaly! It was like me saying, "Help me be more like Jesus" and then snarling in my heart. How sad!!! Can it really be that when my time with God is interrupted I get feisty? I was immediately reminded of Colossians 3:12 RSV, *Put on then, as God's chosen ones, holy and beloved, compassion, kindness, lowliness, meekness, and patience,* There was no kindness and patience at that moment, sad to say. Then God speaks from 1 Peter 3:4 RSV, *but let it be the hidden person of the heart with the imperishable jewel of a gentle and quiet spirit, which in God's sight is very precious.*

Worship is my reaction to His love, my act of kissing God, the most intimate act of love in response to His kisses to me. But worshipping God and then snapping at my husband shows a need for transformation.

I couldn't help but think, *Oh Derry, you have a long way to go!*

Thank you Father for Your tenderness and patience shown through the scriptures that rebuked me and brought me to my senses.

Scripture Kisses:

> Reminder—Be imitators of God.
>
> Put on … kindness … and patience.

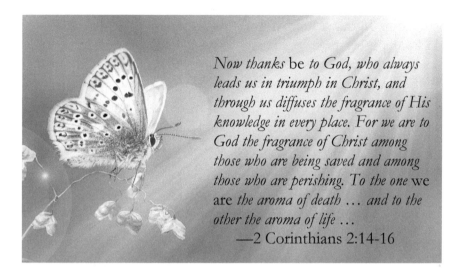

Now thanks be to God, who always leads us in triumph in Christ, and through us diffuses the fragrance of His knowledge in every place. For we are to God the fragrance of Christ among those who are being saved and among those who are perishing. To the one we are the aroma of death ... and to the other the aroma of life ...
—2 Corinthians 2:14-16

Beans

Beans are an interesting thing. They smell so good when they are cooking. Imagine yourself walking into a Mexican restaurant. The fragrance draws you in. You begin looking forward to your meal.

I made a pot of bean soup. It smelled so delicious. I prepared it for a potluck. I carefully packed my crockpot into a box so it would be stable in the car. However, it sloshed! When I arrived at my destination, much of the soup had spilled over onto the carpet of my trunk and all over some of the other items I had stored there.

I wiped them down using tissues I had stored in my car. When I got home I removed things from my trunk and washed the carpet, then brought in some of the things that had been "baptized" with the bean juice and washed them down. I went to the back seat and took out the foot mats that had also received bean juice from moving items from the trunk out of the way.

I thought I had washed everything down. A couple of days later, I opened the car door. I was headed for work. In short, "It stinketh." I couldn't figure out what in the world it was from. It permeated the car so badly that on the way to work—temperatures in the low 20s—I had to open my windows so I could breathe. When I got to work, I could smell that horrible stench on me!

When beans are fresh, the aroma is enticing. When beans are "rotten" they can really stink!

Now I was thinking. There are a number of spiritual lessons we can bring out of this:

- How holding on to a cherished sin can permeate our soul and keep us from being that sweet fragrance of Jesus.

- Or how one negative word or murmuring against someone or something can leave a "stinky residue" on those around. And as it permeates—is shared—a family, a church, an organization can quickly go from being happy, with a beautiful "fragrance" for Christ to a "stinkin'" place to be.

- But today, the point I'll emphasize from the story is the "rottenness" that can grow undetected in us and changes us into people who aren't pleasant to be around when we can't let go of the past.

Those past mistakes, intentional or unintentional, that we hold onto. The regrets that keep us bound in guilt and shame. Those issues that keep us from growing or moving forward—that cause us to hurt, judge or condemn others—sometimes to try to help us feel better about ourselves. That makes us "stink" individually, or just like one bad apple can spoil the bushel so with us one "stinker" can permeates over to our friends or family and can make a "stinkin'" group.

So today, beans equal the importance of forgiving and moving forward. For ourselves and for anyone who is causing us to hold onto an offense, we can be a sweet aroma for Jesus or a "stinkin' presence" that repels others.

Now thanks be to God who always leads us in triumph in Christ, and through us diffuses the fragrance of His knowledge in every place. For we are to God the fragrance of Christ among those who are being saved and among those who are perishing. To the one we are the aroma of death leading to death, and to the other the aroma of life leading to life. And who is sufficient for these things?—2 Corinthians 2:14-16.

God is continually giving us opportunities for new beginnings. One of the important lessons in our spiritual development is learning to release the past so that we can live full in the now, in the presence of God. We all bring the past with us to each new day; but we can choose to take only whatever adds to our enrichment and up-building. We can carry with us the understanding we have gained from our experiences, but let go of the excess baggage of guilt and regret. We are never really able to move forward in the present if we are anchored to the past.

As we let go and look forward, we will gain greater knowledge from each new experience. God is continually giving us new understanding and the opportunity of new beginnings in our life. We need to release ourselves and others from limitations from the past and the mistakes in the past. Choose to let go of yesterday's mistakes and begin anew. Do it now!

Walk in the assurance that when you pass by, you are leaving a sweet aroma for Jesus.

For you were once darkness, but now you are light in the Lord. Walk as children of light—Ephesians 5:8.

But we all, with unveiled face, beholding as in a mirror the glory of the Lord, are being transformed into the same image from glory to glory, just as by the Spirit of the Lord.—2 Corinthians 3:18.

With Kisses From Heaven

This scripture lesson vividly taught me the importance of continuing to strive to be a sweet fragrance that lingers for Jesus, that I might make a difference for the Kingdom of God.

Scripture Kisses:

Be transformed!

Be an aroma for Christ.

if My people who are called by My name will humble themselves, and pray and seek My face, and turn from their wicked ways, then I will hear from heaven, and will forgive their sin and heal their land.
—2 Chronicles 7:14.

And do not be conformed to this world, but be transformed by the renewing of your mind, that you may prove what is that good and acceptable and perfect will of God.—Romans 12:2.

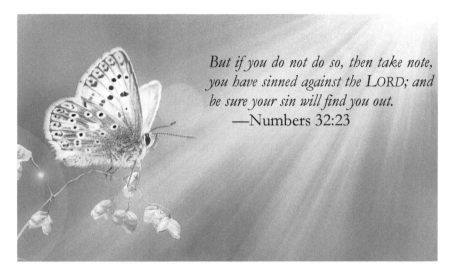

But if you do not do so, then take note, you have sinned against the LORD; and be sure your sin will find you out.
—Numbers 32:23

Big Escape

My sons were really too old to have to take naps, but this day they were asked to lay down on their beds for a while and rest. They had been grumpy and disgruntled all morning. I hoped a quiet timeout would refresh their spirits. I read them a story and told them I would be back to check on them in half an hour.

It became evident that the older of the two was not in agreement with my assessment of their behavior and needs. He was a bold five-year-old who had plans that were different than mine. Usually compliant, I was surprised with his behavior.

After the promised half hour had passed I went upstairs to their room. Hmmm, one was lying there quietly. Where was the other? I looked at my son curiously, "Where's your brother?" I asked. He just looked at me. He wasn't about to squeal on his brother. No response. I followed his eyes but didn't understand. He was looking towards the window. I looked around the room and called his name. No answer. Again I looked at the compliant one. He was not quite four. I followed his gaze—back to the window. I went to the window and looked out. Way down on the other side of the meadow I saw a little black-haired head bobbing through the tall grass.

I noticed the screen was off the window. There was a tree that grew very close to the house. It was taller than this second-story window, but I couldn't believe this little boy could have or would have grabbed hold of the tree and shimmied down. How could he? I must be wrong.

I turned again to the quiet form on the bed. He was in no hurry to get up. I came over to him and gently said, "Son, did your brother climb out the window?" He slowly nodded his head 'yes.'

My next thought was where did he go? I scanned the meadow. Hmmm. Our neighbors lived on the other side. They had children around the ages of my children. Could it be that he went there?

Before I put on my hiking boots, I made a call. When my neighbor answered, I asked, "Do you happen to have a visitor there from our house?"

"Yes. He's sitting here having a bowl of ice cream with us. Did you not know he was here? I asked him when he came in if his mother knew he had come over."

"Thank you. I did not know. Please do not let him finish his ice cream. Please send him directly home."

He was only five. He was old enough to know he was doing wrong but somehow thought he was not going to get caught. He not only got caught but had to suffer the consequences of his decision.

Those reading this book are older and wiser (I hope!), or are there some reading who believe you can do whatever you want and you won't be found out—no one will ever know?

God knows! He is aware of everything concerning you and it matters to Him. He has good things in mind for you. If you are resisting Him, you limit the blessings He is waiting to grant you and His guidance to a better way. I urge you today, confess your sins and get right with God (even if there are some consequences). 1 John 1:9 NIV says, *If we confess our sins, he is faithful and just and will forgive us our sins and purify us from all unrighteousness.*

Note that I said, "Confess to God." We **do** need to confess to others and make things right if we have hurt or offended them. But if your confession would destroy someone else, you'd better check with God to find out whether you need to talk to them. God will direct you somehow. He has many ways of making His will and wisdom known to us.

No matter how tasty your "ice cream" is, it isn't worth it! God promises in Ephesians 3:20 NIV, *Now to him who is able to do immeasurably more than all we ask or imagine, according to his power that is at work within us,* God wants to bless us and do amazing things for us and with us! Put Him first. Do things His way. Experience His love.

Scripture Kiss:

Caught in sin and transformed.

 Butterfly Kiss:

Butterflies are not insects ... They are self-propelled flowers.

—R. A. Heinlein

I will meditate on the glorious splendor of Your majesty, And on Your wondrous works.—Psalm 145:5.

Don't get up. Just sit a while and think. Never be afraid to sit a while and think.

—Asagai to Beneatha, Act III.
Lorraine Hansberry, *A Raisin in the Sun*

And what I say to you, I say to all: Watch!—Mark 13:37

Bird's-Eye View

As a child I used to love to climb this big gnarly tree rooted deeply at the corner of our block right outside our front yard. It was easy to climb and had huge limbs that were comfortable to stretch out on and let your arms and legs hang over.

When I was perched up there no one could see me, but I could watch and hear everything around me. It was a very entertaining and "educating" place to "hang out." Today that makes me think of the verse in Psalm 102:7, *I lie awake, And am like a sparrow alone on the housetop.* I was alone and I had a real bird's-eye view!

I was usually a pretty obedient child, but not when it came to this tree. The tree seemed to beckon me. I would get my chores done quickly and rush out the door disappearing into "my" tree to stand "watch." This didn't please my mother. I was scolded every time she "caught" me. That wasn't often because usually I would hear her calling, "Derry Lee, where are you?" I would quickly come down the tree and enter the house from the backyard.

If I had been old enough at the time to know and understand scripture, a very fitting scripture would have been, Habakkuk 2:1, *I will stand my watch And set myself on the rampart, And watch to see what He will say to me, And what I will answer when I am corrected.* I see now I needed correction for being sneaky and deceptive in my actions. I certainly took my watch and I set myself on the rampart so to speak—a defensive position—waiting to see what I could see and hear … and I would contemplate God and His creation, wonder at His majesty … and then figure out how I would answer if Mom caught me.

Maybe the importance of being attentive and "watchful" became instilled in me as a child from my practice in the tree. I know that as I think back to my childhood "watching" I have been reminded of a number of important scriptures that talk about "watching".

Watch, stand fast in the faith, be brave, be strong.
  —1 Corinthians 16:13.

Therefore let us not sleep, as others do, *but let us watch and be sober.*
  —1 Thessalonians 5:6.

I believe this is telling us not to become slack in our studying God's Word or in our spiritual growth. We are to mature in Jesus, understanding the truths of scripture and His revelations of the future.

Watch therefore, for you do not know what hour your Lord is coming.
  —*Matthew 24:42,*

Watch therefore, and pray always that you may be counted worthy to escape all these things that will come to pass, and to stand before the Son of Man.—Luke 21:36.

God promises He will do nothing without informing us. Amos 3:7 NIV affirms, *Surely the Sovereign LORD does nothing without revealing his plan to his servants the prophets.* That's for us today too. He wants us to be ready for His soon return and we must be "watchful" and pay attention to what He has revealed in His Word.

And then a final warning is found in Revelation 3:3, *Remember therefore how you have received and heard; hold fast and repent. Therefore if you will not watch, I will come upon you as a thief, and you will not know what hour I will come upon you.*

These are all scripture promises, "kisses" from God to keep us in a "ready" mindset—watchful in this world of unrest.

Scripture Kiss:

His love provides direction and answers

For God has not given us a spirit of fear, but of power and of love and of a sound mind.—2 Timothy 1:7.

 Butterfly Kiss:

"Just living is not enough," said the butterfly, "one must have sunshine, freedom, and a little flower."

—Hans Christian Andersen

If you indulge in self-pity, the only sympathy you can expect is from the same source.
　　　—Bill Copeland

This is My commandment, that you love one another as I have loved you.—John 15:12.

Behold, I stand at the door and knock. If anyone hears My voice and opens the door, I will come in to him and dine with him, and he with Me.—Revelation 3:20.

A friend loves at all times, and a brother is born for adversity.
—Proverbs 17:17 NIV

Blood Sisters

Little boys aren't the only ones who like to play cowboys and Indians. Little girls do too, especially when they know they have some trace of American Indian blood in them.

My cousin and younger sister were much more agile than I was, so when we played cowboys and Indians, they were both able to leap over the brick wall or run on top of it before I could even get close to it. It was very exciting for them but after several hours of adventure, I began to feel left out. There was camaraderie between them I was growing jealous of.

I loved my cousin. She was only six months younger than me and I felt I was the one who should have the closer relationship. Together we had all watched the movies that showed how the Indians and White men became blood brothers and how that made them closer friends and family. I decided that was the answer. I would become blood sisters with my cousin.

She thought it was a good idea and we set out to perform our ceremony, hiding from my sister around the side of the house. My cousin was braver than I was. She cut herself and was waiting for me. I was chicken. My idea and I had trouble following through. The pain factor was a bigger issue to me than it was to her. "Hurry up," she ordered, "before my blood dries up. I don't want to have to cut myself again."

My sister heard her, "What are you guys doing?" I had failed to mention to my cousin that this was to be just between us. She immediately spilled the beans. My sister was delighted. She stuck her finger down there so she could be part of it. Before I knew it they had become blood sisters and were off playing while I sat there still trying to be brave enough to cut myself. Since my intentions weren't pure, I probably deserved that!

As I reflected back on this experience, God's family came to mind. I remembered Jesus questioning His disciples when they came to Him and told Him that His mother and brother were there to see Him. Matthew 12:46-50 NIV says, *While Jesus was still talking to the crowd, his mother and brothers stood outside, wanting to speak to him. Someone told him, "Your mother and brothers are standing outside, wanting to speak to you." He replied to him, "Who is my mother, and who are my brothers?" Pointing to his disciples, he said, "Here are my mother and my brothers. For whoever does the will of my Father in heaven is my brother and sister and mother."* He wasn't denying them, He was saying my family is made up of those who believe in me.

Who are the children of God? Are they the natural children or the ones that believe? God has adopted us into His family through Jesus if we believe on Him. Can God's family members have a closer bond with us than our biological family? Yes, it is possible that we can have a closer bond with members of God's family than with our biological family. The unity that occurs doesn't take a "blood sister" ceremony, but it does take believing in the shed "blood" of our Lord and Savior Jesus.

In John 17:20-23 NIV, Jesus offered a beautiful prayer on our behalf, He prayed to His Heavenly Father, our Father in heaven. *My prayer is not for them alone.* [His disciples] *I pray also*

almost anything to have us share His Heavenly home. Jesus sacrificed much for us. God is on our team. He doesn't set us up for failure. He wants us to come out victorious. He's with us to help that happen.

Prayer is a special mode of communication that has been provided for our frequent use. At no additional charge we can take advantage of this opportunity anytime. day or night, wherever our location. No special equipment is required.

Just as our cell phones need to be recharged so do we. Our bonus is when our battery is low, God still picks up our signal. When we realize human wisdom is insufficient and our effectiveness is dependent upon Gods' rejuvenating power, we will be eager to communicate with Him through His gift of prayer.

But the end of all things is at hand: be ye therefore sober, and watch unto prayer.—1 Peter 4:7 KJV

Because of this scripture lesson, I pray more often with a desire to keep in continual communication with heaven.

(For further instruction on prayer, please refer to my Living series—*Praying in the "Yes" of God* and *Growing in the "Yes" of God.*)

Scripture Kiss:

God wants to talk to us and listens when we pray.

But the Lord is faithful, who will establish you and guard you from the evil one.—2 Thessalonians 3:3.

God is your strength and He alone is the victor. The stress and performance of the battle rests in the Lord, not on your physical skill or strength.

—Author unknown

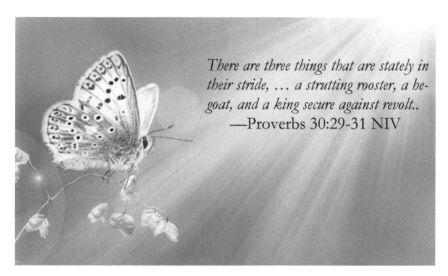

There are three things that are stately in their stride, ... a strutting rooster, a he-goat, and a king secure against revolt..
—Proverbs 30:29-31 NIV

Chicken Protector

I grew up in California where I lived all my life until 2010. I started out in southern California and then in my middle 20s moved to northern California. My mother moved just shortly before I did, but she moved to Oregon. It had been well over a year since I had seen her. It was a long trip but we were on our way.

Mom was never much for traveling long distances and visiting but her home was open if you could get to her. She had described her new home over the phone. She said she was way out in the country on 80 acres. They had horses, goats, peacocks and chickens.

It was hard to imagine my mother this way. When I was growing up she had an executive position. I can remember her getting ready for work all spiffed up in her dress suit, hair in a French roll.

I can't ever remember my mother with her hair down and loose, so when we got to the end of this long country driveway and I saw a woman standing on the deck of the house there, I didn't recognize her. Even when she waved, I wondered where we were and if we had taken a wrong turn.

With Kisses From Heaven

Mom was excited to see us and came down the steps headed our way. Only when I got close enough to her did I recognize her features. Hair down and laughing, she grabbed me and hugged me. She was eager to show me around the place. We took a few minutes to unload the car and bring our things into their home. What a great view of the mountains across the ridge!

"Come on," she invited. "You've been cooped up in the car for hours. Let's go for a walk and I'll show you around."

While we were on our walk a rooster and two hens crossed the road in front of us. Suddenly Mom stopped and said, "Watch this." Then she yelled, "Duke, he's after your girls again." She no sooner got the words out of her mouth when a big rooster flew out of the tree squawking and flapping its wings headed straight for the rooster that had just crossed the driveway with three hens. He was out to protect his own and he retrieved his ladies! That was a quick response.

I was stunned. Not only had my mother "let her hair down," but she was talking to the animals and they listened to her. He came immediately to protect his hens.

Reflecting on this story made me think of Jesus who said in Luke 13:34, *How often I wanted to gather your children to-gether, as a hen* gathers *her brood under* her *wings, but you were not willing!* Jesus wants so much to protect us and care for us but we, unlike Duke, don't always respond quickly, if at all, when the Holy Spirit speaks to us. But if we listen and are willing, He promises:

He shall cover you with His feathers, And under His wings you shall take refuge; His truth shall be your shield and buckler.—Psalm 91:4.

And then He assures:

But let all who take refuge in you be glad; let them ever sing for joy. Spread your protection over them, that those who love your name may rejoice in you.—Psalm 5:11 NIV.

Scripture Kisses:

God's creation has many lessons for us if we are watchful and attentive.

God's invitations for us to take refuge in Him.

A man is never in worse company than when he flies into a rage and is beside himself!
—Author unknown

He shall call upon Me, and I will answer him; I will be *with him in trouble; I will deliver him and honor him. With long life I will satisfy him, And show him My salvation.*—Psalm 91:15-16.

Aunt Jean at her 100th birthday party with her
brothers Pasquale, 99 at left , and Papa Mario, 92.
Blessed with long life!

Each of us wages a private battle each day between the grand fantasies we have for ourselves and what actually happens.
 —Cathy Guisewite

... and take every thought captive to obey Christ,
　　　　　—2 Corinthians 10:5 RSV

Christmas Burglar

Christmas was always a special time for our family. Mom made it that way. She never failed to have the place warmly decorated and inviting. This year all the family was gathering at our house; grandparents, uncles, aunts, and cousins. We had a very small home and I wondered where mother was going to put them all. But she was not at all concerned. She had it figured out. The children would give up their beds for the aunties. Grandma would share my mother's bed with her. All of the men and children would claim a piece of floor in the living room and hunker down for the night.

It is usually difficult for children to settle down to sleep when there is so much activity and laughter around them, so we were allowed to stay up until the grownups went to bed.

My uncles were out like a light in no time. Their snoring kept me awake. I was only ten and wasn't used to so much noise. I finally relaxed and fell asleep.

I don't know what time it was when I awoke startled. The room was dark. I could hear snoring and quiet breathing, but over those sounds I heard a rattle and scraping against the living room window which was directly in front of me. The moon was out and I could see a shadow—movement outside

39

the window. I froze. I was terrified. I couldn't speak out. I couldn't move. All I could do is lay there and watch—in panic!

I watched and waited. Again, more movement. My vigil kept up all night. I couldn't sleep. I lay there trembling and waiting…and finally praying with my heart pounding. Every now and then I would see movement and hear the noise. I tried to tell myself nobody was out there, but it wasn't working. I tried to believe that maybe it was a bush moving in the wind, but I couldn't think of any bush that was high enough to be seen in the window.

Finally as dusk was filtering through the window, I dozed off. When I was awakened with my cousins giggling I got up, dressed and headed cautiously outside to investigate. Sure enough, it had been a bush moving with the wind.

As I think back to that experience it makes me think of the verse in 2 Corinthians 10:5 KJV, *Casting down imaginations, and every high thing that exalteth itself against the knowledge of God, and bringing into captivity every thought to the obedience of Christ;*

The enemy wants to take control of our minds and bring us duress. Some adults have difficulty with satan pulling down their thoughts and causing them all kinds of anxiety and questions. It can even be difficult for an adult who knows Jesus to keep a clear head sometimes.

The enemy will deceive us any way he possibly can. It is important that we know God's Word and that we use it as a weapon against the attacks of the enemy. God directs us in Psalm 19:14 *Let the words of my mouth and the meditation of my heart Be acceptable in Your sight, O LORD, my strength and my Redeemer.* We need to be aware of what we let our hearts meditate upon, so that our mind is stayed on Christ Jesus. The Bible becomes more real as we find it reliable.

Scripture Kiss:

The revelation to a little girl that the devil wants to cause fear but she can turn to Jesus and find peace. He is near.

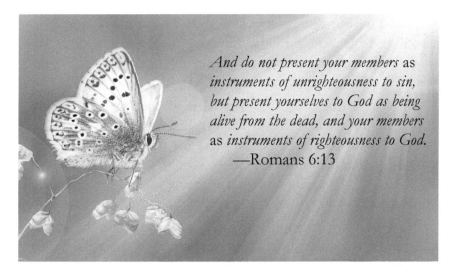

And do not present your members as instruments of unrighteousness to sin, but present yourselves to God as being alive from the dead, and your members as instruments of righteousness to God.
—Romans 6:13

Cigarette Smashing

In my family of origin, I was the oldest of five children, four sisters and the youngest my brother. My name Derry was a derivative of my dad's name, "Derwent." It was his nickname. Male or female, the first born was to be "Derry."

My dad died when I was a sophomore in high school. Mom worked hard to keep things going. It also meant that as the oldest I had to keep things going in the house after school until she got home from work. Sometimes that meant getting dinner started, other times it was household chores. If things were done ahead and my homework was finished I had free time.

There was a young man named Mike who lived down the block from us whose parents also worked. We all hung out together...usually with him at our house. He was older and wiser, so he taught us many important things, like how to make a Dagwood sandwich. Unfortunately although we thoroughly enjoyed it, a week's worth of sandwich fixings were used up at one sitting. That didn't go over very well with Mom, but she was tolerant because someone older was with us in her absence and we weren't entirely alone every day.

So we all grew up together, until I went off to boarding school and he went into the military. We kept in touch. My family remained in that house for a few more years before moving.

The summer after my first year of college, I was living in an apartment across from the hospital where I had a summer job. I was doing secretarial work for the Chaplain there. I received a letter announcing Mike would be home on leave and was eager to catch up with me. He let me know when he would be in town and when to expect a visit.

I was rooming with my college roommate at the apartment and we decided to make him something special for dinner. Then I had a thought. I needed her help with it.

Mike smoked cigarettes. It used to upset Mom and she would demand that he not smoke around us, but sometimes he hid around the house and did. I got the brilliant idea that I wanted him to know I had grown up. I decided I better learn to smoke *fast*. My roommate and I went out and bought some cigarettes. We didn't want anyone we knew to see us smoking so we took a long walk far away from where we lived to practice looking proficient.

I held a cigarette just so and asked her if I looked like I knew what I was doing. She had some suggestions. Then I tried different things like blowing it through my nose or making circle puffs. We worked on this for a couple of hours and then satisfied, headed back to the apartment.

The plan was, when he knocked at the door, she would answer. I would run into the bedroom, light up and come out of the room taking a drag on the ciggie. We practiced that too. Things were looking good.

The next afternoon, there was a knock at the door. The plan went into action. I came around the corner taking a long drag on the freshly lit cigarette, squealing hello and running to hug him. He grabbed me and gave me a kiss. I followed it with, "So good to see you." and put the cigarette in my mouth in front of him so he couldn't miss it.

Before I knew what was happening he took the palm of his hand and ground the cigarette between my teeth. I shrieked and ran for the bathroom. Over the sink I went, spitting and coughing, scooping water into my mouth to rid myself of the horrible matter stuck between my teeth. Now I'm crying and humiliated.

Mike came in behind me and put his hand on my shoulder. "I told you I never wanted any sister of mine to smoke. It's a horrible habit and especially unappealing for a young lady. I don't ever want to see you with a cigarette in your mouth again!"

Despite all the embarrassment, Mike did me a great favor. I never picked up another cigarette or have even been tempted to smoke.

Once I became a Christian, I was thankful I didn't have something else to overcome. When I learned the scripture in 1 Corinthians 9:27, *But I discipline my body and bring it into subjection, lest, when I have preached to others, I myself should become disqualified.* I realized the necessity of taking control of my body and not let my bodily cravings control me. A number of scriptures make it clear that we have an obligation to care for the body God has given us. That means what we put into it and how we care for it.

Or do you not know that your body is the temple of the Holy Spirit who is in you, whom you have from God, and you are not your own? For you were bought at a price; therefore glorify God in your body and in your spirit, which are God's.—1 Corinthians 6:19-20.

Do you not know that you are the temple of God and that the Spirit of God dwells in you? If anyone defiles the temple of God, God will destroy him. For the temple of God is holy, which temple you are.
—1 Corinthians 3:16-17.

With Kisses From Heaven

I beseech you therefore, brethren, by the mercies of God, that you present your bodies a living sacrifice, holy, acceptable to God, which is your reasonable service.—Romans 12:1.

The importance we put on caring for what God has entrusted to us is also expressed by worshipping Him with it.

Scripture Kiss:

Mike's visit and protective correction. Long before I knew these scriptures, Mike set me up for living them out in my life, which helped me honor God's instructions. Our body belongs to God and we must take care of it … and treat it tenderly.

 Butterfly Kiss:

Butterflies can't see their wings. They can't see how truly beautiful they are, but everyone else can. People are like that as well.

—Naya Rivera

Nevertheless let each one of you in particular so love his own wife as himself, and let the wife see that she respects her husband.
—Ephesians 5:33

Circle Of Love And Honor

This text gives such definite direction. Husbands are admonished to love their wives and wives are admonished to respect their husbands. Have you given that much thought?

Men, when a woman feels loved and we feel we're the most important thing in the world to our man, we will do almost anything for him. When we feel loved, it makes it so much easier to show our man respect, even though we know respect is not optional. Love is expressed as a commitment. Jesus gave us that example on the cross. Commitment helps a woman feel secure.

Ladies, do you realize that if we show respect and honor to our husbands it's much easier for them to love and cherish us? When your man doesn't show you he cares about you as a person or if you have no voice with him, or he makes you feel like your ideas, desires, happiness or dreams don't matter, it is difficult to show respect, but it is the right thing to do—even when your husband acts selfishly. Colossians 3:18 says, *Wives, submit to your own husbands, as is fitting in the Lord.*

Gentlemen, when your woman is acting like other things are more important than you, uncaring, when she is belligerent or sarcastic, it's difficult to reach out lovingly, but it's the right thing to do—even when she is acting defensively. 1 Peter 3:7 cautions, *Husbands, likewise, dwell with* them *with under-standing, giving honor to the wife, as to the weaker vessel, and as* being *heirs together of the grace of life, that your prayers may not be hindered.*

One feeds the other as it forms a continuous circle. If that circle of love isn't working in your home, somebody has to mend it. So men, either you're each going to need to start loving your wife so she can respect you, or ladies you're each going to have to start respecting your husband so he can love you more. Somebody's got to break the cycle and mend the circle of love. I guess the real question is: How much do we really want a happy marriage, a content and satisfying relationship? Do we want it enough to humble ourselves and make the necessary changes or would we rather wallow in our pride and misery? We may need to extend mercy to each other as well as forgiveness.

The Bible tells us that we can approach God at the throne of grace with boldness in Hebrews 4:16, *Let us therefore come boldly to the throne of grace, that we may obtain mercy and find grace to help in time of need.* His arms are open to us. He wants us to turn to Him for help. He wants to help us! No matter what wrong we have done, He extends mercy and grace to us. If we are to become more like Jesus and do things His way, we need to follow His example—show each other mercy and grace.

What does "mercy" mean? I looked it up in a dictionary. There were many definitions: compassion, pity, love, forgiveness, kindness, sympathy, tolerance, generosity, tenderheartedness. There is much God is willing to pour out on us—or open to us—however you want to look at it, if we are willing to come to Him. How would it be in our relationships if we saturated our partner with all the components of mercy?

If you feel you are always the one giving in or soothing the wounds, stand in faith. Proverbs 18:22 RSV says, *He who finds a wife finds a good thing, and obtains favor from the LORD.* Let your confession be: "My husband has found a good thing and

I am that good thing." Then do what you need to do to be that "good thing" with God's help.

Scripture Kisses:

These scriptures reminded me of how important marriage is to the Lord. He gives us the formula for a happy marriage, if we are just willing to heed His instructions. It isn't that difficult if we let God work through us and enable us to do our part in strengthening and healing our relationships. We can adhere without reservation and reap immeasurable rewards. In fact, the closer we grow to God, the closer we grow to each other—like a triangle with God at the top point. We grow more like Him and it closes the gap between us, filling both with a light and joyful heart. Put on Jesus!

If your marriage can use an extra boost, I encourage you to consider taking a marriage education class at one of your local churches that provide such instruction, or contact me and we will assist you.

As soon as the lad had gone, David arose from a place toward the south, fell on his face to the ground, and bowed down three times. And they kissed one another; and they wept together, but David more so.
—1 Samuel 20:41

As a tree planted by the river flourishes, the waters of God are the promises from which you can continually draw comfort.

> —Author unknown. 1992 Prayer Journal, Promise.

And God will wipe away every tear from their eyes; there shall be no more death, nor sorrow, nor crying. There shall be no more pain, for the former things have passed away." Then He who sat on the throne said, "Behold, I make all things new." And He said to me, "Write, for these words are true and faithful."—Revelation 21:4-5

Community Grieves

It was a beautiful day. The fairgrounds were open and the Fair was about to begin. Families had been gathering since early morning in preparation. People were shouting greetings across the fairgrounds to one another. Laughter was in the air. Excited children were running around, enjoying each others' company, fully engrossed in their play.

At the livestock arena, two families arrived together. They were in a large truck with a number of items to unload. The driver stopped to receive instructions, and in that short moment one of the young boys jumped on the back of the truck. When the truck started moving, it lurched, throwing the child onto the road. Before anyone even knew he was there, the driver, backing up, ran over the small boy.

This precious little guy was immediately taken to the hospital, but was found dead on arrival. As the hospital chaplain, I was called to the Emergency Room to meet the family as they arrived. When the child's mother heard the news, she fell on the floor wailing, writhing in pain, clutching the floor, and screaming. None of us knew what to do.

My heart was breaking as I witnessed her anguish. I lay down on the floor, on my back, next to her, and took her in my arms and held her. She sobbed and sobbed, hanging on to me for dear life.

When she was ready, we transitioned her to where her son was. She grabbed him up and took him in her arms sobbing, and stroking him. Throughout the hospital, in various waiting areas were shocked neighbors, family and friends.

This mom held and rocked her son for almost four hours. It was obvious that she was not about to part with her precious child. As I experienced her desperation, I finally asked her neighbor to go to this mother's home and bring back her son's favorite blanket and toy. When she returned with them, I helped the mother wrap her son in the blanket and told her that it was almost time for her to leave him with me. I reminded her it was God's desire for her to be reunited with him one day in heaven.

About an hour later she placed him in my arms and wound up his stuffed toy asking me to keep winding it up until they came to take him away.

Heartache, grief, disappointment, we all face these in many ways, small and large, sometimes daily. We can do it alone or we can turn to the Comforter.

Whoever you are, if you find yourself in any difficult situation ask God for wisdom and know He will send help to see you through. If you are around the brokenhearted, be willing to do whatever it takes to minister to them. Share the journey with those experiencing loss. Words are not as necessary as your presence and your love.

God admonishes us in 1 Thessalonians 4:18, 17 *Therefore comfort one another with these words. Then we who are alive and remain shall be caught up together with them in the clouds to meet the Lord in the air. And thus we shall always be with the Lord.*

Scripture Kiss:

God extends His love and comfort through us if we are willing. Let God show His love through you.

Hold Fast True Riches

Let me hold lightly things of this earth;
Transient treasures, what are they worth?
Moths can corrupt them, rust can decay;
All their bright beauty fades in a day.
Let me hold lightly temporal things—
I, who am deathless, I, who wear wings!

Let me hold fast, Lord, things of the skies,
Quicken my vision, open my eyes!
Show me Thy riches, glory and grace,
Boundless as time is, endless as space …
Let me hold lightly things that are mine—
Lord, Thou dost give me all that is Thine!
    —Martha Snell Nicholson

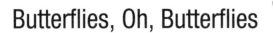

Butterflies, Oh, Butterflies

Butterflies, Oh, Butterflies,
Your beauty is so rare.
Butterflies, Oh, butterflies,
How could anyone dare
to catch you and to hold you
against your solemn will?
They should just admire you
and let you have your fill
of flitting here and flitting there,
gathering up your daily fare
of nectars from the flowers bright,
from early morning until night.
Butterflies, beautiful butterflies,
with so many colours rare,
it hurts my heart when one dies,
yet, does anyone truly care?
For butterflies, butterflies,
you represent new birth,
from chrysalis until you die,
you beautify the earth.
Thank you, lovely butterflies.
                —Author unknown

A righteous man *regards the life of his animal, …*—Proverbs 12:10

Since his days are *determined, The number of his months* is *with You; You have appointed his limits, so that he cannot pass.*—Job 14:5

CPR On My Pomeranian

My little dog had died. I was sad but I knew that though my heart was grieving I couldn't go around sulking. That wouldn't set a good example for my sons. She was my dog but the boys missed her too.

About two months later I was called into the kitchen. My second oldest son Brian had a little box on the floor. He asked me to open it. When I looked inside I found the most adorable little blonde and white Pomeranian. He smiled and said, "She's for you, Mom."

What really made her special was the story behind her. Shortly after my little dog had died, Brian started looking for another dog for me. When he saw this Pomeranian he was sure I would love her. He asked his dad if they could get it for me. His dad told him he had never paid for a dog and wasn't going to now. Brian urged then begged. Finally his dad told him if he wanted to get it for me he would have to earn the money.

Now I understood why Brian had taken over the kitchen for the last month or so baking bread. He was selling it to neighbors and parents from the local school; anywhere he could get a sale. Day after day he was baking bread.

With Kisses From Heaven

I knew he was selling it but was under the impression he was saving up for something *he* wanted. I had no idea all this effort was to get me a dog.

She was a very special little dog too. I named her "Little Bit." She followed me everywhere.

By the time we moved into the garage while we were building, Little Bit had become a faithful and very protective friend. If I got up in the middle of the night, she followed me.

Once when I came down with the flu and was very ill, running a high fever, I decided to put a blanket down outside and get some sunshine and fresh air. Little Bit came along and lay down on the blanket next to me. I woke up with ants crawling on me...big ants. I was very weak but I started sweeping them off the blanket with my hand. Little Bit watched me and started pushing them off with her nose. She was an attentive little companion.

Not long after, we were outside and the boys were playing baseball. One hard-hit baseball missed its mark, but hit Little Bit and knocked her unconscious. At first we thought she was dead. She had flipped over and her feet were in the air. She wasn't moving. My husband ran over, cupped her muzzle in his hands and began CPR on my Pomeranian. I prayed—hard, asking God to breathe life into her. She lived!!!

She was never quite the same after that. She started acting a bit strange, but even more protective of me. She had never been a yapper; never chased cars; always stayed by my side...until one day. For no understandable reason, Little Bit decided to chase my girlfriend's car as she was leaving. But she ran for the car from the side and ended up under the tires as my friend was driving away. There was no saving her.

Thinking about this unexpected turn of events for Little Bit is a reminder that we plan for tomorrow but we do not know what tomorrow holds. James 4:13-16 reminds us, *Come now, you who say, "Today or tomorrow we will go to such and such a city, spend a year there, buy and sell, and make a profit"; whereas you do not know what* will happen *tomorrow. For what is your life? It is even a*

54

vapor that appears for a little time and then vanishes away. Instead you ought *to say, "If the Lord wills, we shall live and do this or that." But now you boast in your arrogance. All such boasting is evil* Our destiny is in God's hands and we need to make the best of every day of life He gives us.

There are many plans in a man's heart, Nevertheless the LORD'S *counsel—that will stand.*—Proverbs 19:21.

This is no reason to fear. Our God loves us. He desires that we spend eternity with Him. Our calling on this earth is to love Him and share His love with others. In this story, Brian did that for me. He shared his time, his energy and his love to bless me. And bless me he did. His story sets a good example for us, how we can devote a little effort to bless someone and bring happiness into their life.

Thinking of my girlfriend and what happened, I thought of Jesus' example to extend mercy—the same mercy and grace we desire to have extended to us when we mess up. It was many, many months before she would learn what had happened that day.

We need to give each other grace and be patient with one another. Better it would be if we encouraged each other and helped each other move into a transition of being more like our Jesus. None of us is perfect. None of us has wings or a halo yet.

God has numbered our days. We need to do our best and give God our best.

LORD, *make me to know my end, And what* is *the measure of my days, That I may know how frail I am. Indeed, You have made my days* as *handbreadths, And my age is as nothing before You; Certainly every man at his best state* is *but vapor. Selah Surely every man walks about like a shadow; Surely they busy themselves in vain; He heaps up* riches, *And does not know who will gather them. "And now, Lord, what do I wait for? My hope* is *in You.*—Psalm 39:4-7.

With Kisses From Heaven

I have a bumper sticker that says, "Make a good day!" It was a favorite saying of my friend and supervisor, Shoushan Salibian. That is always good advice. We can determine the tone of the day by choosing how we will respond to what a day offers. Will we make it a good day—for ourself and others?

Scripture Kiss:

A reminder to live each day as though it were our last, giving our best to each other.

This is *the day the* LORD *has made; We will rejoice and be glad in it.*
—Psalm 118:24.

 Butterfly Kiss:

Perhaps the butterfly is proof that you can go through a great deal of darkness yet still become something beautiful.

—Beau Taplin

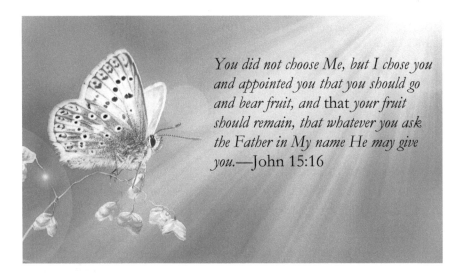

You did not choose Me, but I chose you and appointed you that you should go and bear fruit, and that your fruit should remain, that whatever you ask the Father in My name He may give you.—John 15:16

For Him

Sitting at the terminal, I found myself alone and a bit emotional. This visit with my children had been exceptionally wonderful. I had had an opportunity to go shopping for maternity clothes with my daughter-in-love (not -in-law), who was expecting their first child, a rare privilege indeed since I lived in California and they were living in Canada. I had come up early to visit them before we all attended a Bible Conference.

To my surprise my son, pastor of his first congregation, invited me to spend the following day with him as he conducted a Bible study and did visitations.

He closed our day together by taking us all on an evening canoe trip. The choir of birds was unbelievable. I thoroughly enjoyed listening to birds singing their goodnight songs and going canoeing around dusk. The perfect close to a perfect day.

My range of activities had been greatly reduced due to a knee injury and I was finding it painfully difficult to get around the airport. I sat there reflecting on the events of the past few days. There had been several opportunities to encourage and support the young people attending the conference in their decision for the Lord.

One young lady was staying at my son's home to commute to the conference. We were sharing a room and each night there was some deep heart-to-heart communication and prayer that went on between us. One of the most powerful things we can do is share our personal testimony.

You can imagine how thrilled I was the next day when a call was made to receive Jesus Christ as one's Lord and Savior at the evening meeting and she and my grandson responded.

It was directly after the closing song that I had a strong impression in my heart to head to the ladies washroom immediately. Within seconds three girls entered in tears. Now, if you hadn't responded to God's call, but your heart had been moved to the point of tears from your turmoil, where would you run to hide if you were a girl? Ladies room—right?

Mother that I am, it didn't take long to engage them in conversation. After pouring out their hearts we formed a prayer circle, right there, right then. They gave their hearts to Jesus and turned their lives over to Him. Another unexpected blessing!

When I signed up for this conference, I had the idea it was over a day earlier than it was. It would not have made any difference as far as my schedule was concerned because I had a two-day mandatory training program I had to attend at the hospital the following day. Because of my error, I was concerned that my children would have to miss several hours of the continuing workshops to take me to the airport.

I did some checking for shuttle service but to no avail. I began praying. The Lord already had a plan. My sweet young roommate inquired about my departure. I shared with her what I had just been mulling over. She said, "No problem. I think my mom is free that day and would love to get better acquainted with you." That's exactly what happened.

Another new friend, and since she was one of my son's parishioners I had the opportunity to find out what a terrific pastor he was and what a great job he was doing.

I started this trip home once again asking God to use me throughout the day. While waiting for the second leg of my flight I learned a woman and her adult daughter were on their way to support her 36-year-old son. He had been in a serious accident and was facing amputation of his leg. We concluded our visit with time in prayer for him.

Jesus has called us to share His love with others, to be His disciples and make disciples. Matthew 28:19-20, *Go there-fore and make disciples of all the nations, baptizing them in the name of the Father and of the Son and of the Holy Spirit, teaching them to ob-serve all things that I have commanded you; and lo, I am with you al-ways,* even *to the end of the age. Amen.*

Turning our life and time over to Jesus opens opportu-nities for rewarding ministry. Working for and with Jesus pro-vides many exciting episodes to life. This trip to Canada held multiple blessings and surprises!

Scripture Kiss:

Walking in the calling of these scriptures opens doors of adventure and fulfillment.

God is never too busy to care about the small things in our lives. All the small things add to our faith. If these small things thrill us, how much more will Heaven enthrall us?
—Dorothy Matthews

For the sorrow that is according to the will of *God produces a repentance without regret,* leading *to salvation,* ...
—2 Corinthians 7:10 NASB.

Whatever your present situation, view it in the light of what God is teaching you, through circumstances, about Himself and you will come to know God in dimensions you have never known Him before.

—Henry Blackaby, *Experiencing God,* p210

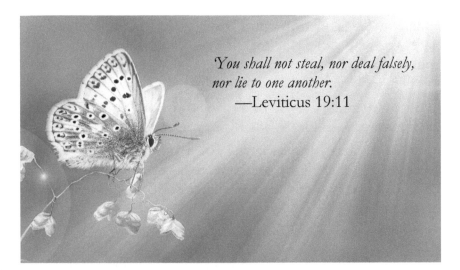

*'You shall not steal, nor deal falsely,
nor lie to one another.*
—Leviticus 19:11

Forbidden Flowers

Flowers are beautiful. God made them in a magnificent array of colors, shapes and sizes. I've always loved flowers. I love flowers of any color and any type, except carnations. I'm not as crazy about sweet, sweet-smelling carnations or super fragrant lilies. They along with daffodils can give me a headache and make me a bit nauseous. Any other flower works for me with no problem. God knows how much I love them and there was a time in my life He made sure I had fresh flowers for over a year. You can read that story in my book *With Gladness Every Day*.

We had recently moved into a new neighborhood. The old house was new to us. We hadn't met our neighbors yet but I was, as a little eight-year-old girl, excited to have the neighbors we had living next to us. Why? Because all along the side of their house that was next to ours, they had planted beautiful flowering plants. She had a beautiful flower garden of many varieties and assorted colors. I would walk around the house so I could enjoy looking at them and smelling them.

A few weeks after we had moved in Mother was busy in the kitchen. I snuck up behind her and pulled on her apron. She turned around and looked at me. I smiled sweetly and extended my fist—full of beautiful flowers. Mother looked me in the eyes, then looked at the flowers. She took them gently from my hand and thanked me. She said, "Let's get a vase to put these in."

Mom and I put the flowers in a vase and then she knelt down to my level. "Derry, where did you get these flowers?"

In my heart I must have known I had done something wrong, because when she asked me that question, I could feel my face flush. "I got them on the side of the house. I answered honestly.

"Do you mean you got them from the neighbor's plants?" she quizzed.

"Well yes, I suppose, but they were hanging out." I quietly responded.

"What does Jesus tell us about taking something that doesn't belong to us?"

"We're not supposed too."

"What do you think you should do about this?"

"I don't know."

"Perhaps it's time for you to meet our neighbor. Maybe you need to go next door and let her know what you did."

"Oh Mommy, no! I can't do that."

"Who took the flowers?"

"I did"

"Who should talk to the neighbors then?"

"I guess me."

"Hmmm. Why don't you go take care of it now so you can get this off your mind?"

"What do I say?"

"Do you think telling her you're sorry would be a good place to start?"

"I suppose"

And so I did. I was forgiven and met with a kind response from our neighbor.

Isaiah 30:15 NASB says, *For thus the Lord GOD, the Holy One of Israel, has said, "In repentance and rest you will be saved, In quietness and trust is your strength."* ... That seems to sum up my experience as a child.—I repented because my trust was in Jesus. I rested in Him and He gave me the strength and courage to confront my neighbor.

Mother taught us morals and ethics at a young age, and she modeled what she taught us.

Now as an adult I hear and see so many people who wink at "stealing" small things or keeping something that doesn't belong to them, or bringing things home from work that they believe they need at home more than at work. God doesn't put a monetary value on His command to not steal. He simply says, "Don't." He is very clear about His unhappiness with liars. They won't be in heaven. Revelation 21:8 tells us, *But the cowardly, unbelieving, abominable, murderers, sexually immoral, sorcerers, idolaters, and all liars shall have their part in the lake which burns with fire and brimstone, which is the second death."*

Let's keep our consciences clear and be watchful that we don't intentionally or unintentionally take off with something belonging to someone else or cover anything we do with a deceitful or untruthful word. Picking forbidden flowers and walking out the consequences nurtured in me the importance of respecting other people's property and admitting my wrongs; but there are many other "sins" mentioned in that verse. Know that God will forgive any and all if we repent and confess.

Let him who stole steal no longer, but rather let him labor, working with his hands what is good, that he may have something to give him who has need.—Ephesians 4:28.

Lying lips are an abomination to the LORD, But those who deal truthfully are His delight.—Proverbs 12:22.

With Kisses From Heaven

Scripture Kiss:

Doing things Jesus' way brings peace, a clear conscience and a pure heart.

The LORD appeared to us in the past, saying: "I have loved you with an everlasting love; I have drawn you with unfailing-kindness.
—Jeremiah 31:3 NIV.

History is the record of an encounter between character and circumstance.

—Donald Creighton

Like clouds and wind without rain is one who boasts of gifts never given.
—Proverbs 25:14 NIV

Forgotten Horse

I was living at a place where I was caretaking three children besides my own. The family I worked for owned a horse that had been bred. The second oldest son was looking forward to the birth because it would become his very own. I was excited for him.

I loved horses and had always wanted my own horse. The neighbors had a young filly that hadn't been broken yet. They were often away so no one was working this horse. She didn't seem to get much attention.

Since their paddock shared our fence line, I became good friends with this horse. I tamed it, of sorts. When we first met it acted wild and untrusting. Pretty soon she was coming over to the fence when I approached, waiting for me to stroke her face, rub her ears, and give her a carrot treat. She was a beautiful chestnut horse with a white blaze down the front of her face. My love for her continued to grow.

The neighbors had no objection to me befriending her. Actually, I think they were relieved that she was getting attention they were unable to give her. That was verified when about six months later, I was asked if I wanted the horse. The neighbors were willing to just give me the horse. This would provide better care for their horse and was an investment in my happiness and an answer to the longings of my heart.

The family I had been living with was moving. We were invited to move with them so I could continue to care for the children. The home where we would be moving had plenty of room for the horses. I eagerly anticipated finally having my own horse and living in a place that had riding trails and an excellent training area. This new house was about an hour from where we were presently living. We had to make a number of trips to transfer all the household possessions and outside equipment. The last to come would be the horses. I had been told that "my" horse was welcome and I didn't have to worry about how it was going to get there.

The horse trailer wasn't big enough to haul all the horses at one time so I waited until the next trip.

The next trip didn't come. I asked if we could work it out to bring "my" horse. The response was "We'll see what we can do." But my horse was forgotten.

Let's shorten the story. I never did get my horse. My heart was broken and trust suffered because a promise to me had been broken, with no reason or concern for my feelings.

I have learned to trust God in all things. I have also learned we don't always get what we want. When we go through disappointments, God has reasons. That doesn't mean there won't be tears or heartache. It just means God loves us so much He sometimes has to let us be disappointed because He can see what is ahead. With the twists and turns my life took, the horse would have become an expense and hardship I would not have been able to handle. The pain of separation would have been far worse the longer I had invested myself into her.

I am thankful I trusted God and let go of any resentment. This experience reminded me how important it is to keep our word and when we break our word, we often wound relationships and cause distrust.

but whoever keeps his word, in him truly love for God is perfected. By this we may be sure that we are in him:—1 John 2:5 RSV.

Scripture Kiss:

We are reminded of how important it is to God for us to keep our word. When we do, it fosters a sense of trust and confidence.

he sent forth his word, and healed them, and delivered them from destruction.—Psalm 107:20 RSV.

Strength is lost if your attitude of thanksgiving is diminished … A thankless heart today can forfeit the blessings of the future.

—Author unknown

Then Jesus said to him, "Get up! Pick up your mat and walk."
—John 5:8 NIV

Fractured Tailbone

As I slipped and took a trip down the flight of stairs, my bottom didn't miss a step until I came to an abrupt stop at the end of the landing. I managed to hit my back, shoulders and head as I attempted to grab the railing and stop myself. The next day I slept all day. Around 3:15 I woke up with a surge through me. The next day an x-ray verified I had a fractured tailbone.

The following Sunday I was attending a women's conference. The ladies prayed over me. During their prayers they saw a funnel of light encircle me.

On the way home I "happened upon" a doctor who worked in Rehab helping people recover from surgery and accidents. Several items were suggested for me to pick up at a health food store. I followed through, but found the items I needed were not available. While I was shopping God sent a masseuse who offered help and shared what she found effective. She shared with me the same suggestions she gave her clients.

I had been originally told I would be out of work for months. I was back to work on the following Thursday. Was that circle of light the healing presence of God? It seems so.

With Kisses From Heaven

God has so many ways of reaching out His healing touch to us. Sometimes He does it in a way that will instruct us so we can instruct and bless others. The bible tells us in John 14:26, *But the Helper, the Holy Spirit, whom the Father will send in My name, He will teach you all things, and bring to your remembrance all things that I said to you.*

Thank You for fusing together my fractured tailbone and for Your gift and promises of healing and restoration, Thank You for educating me in ways to help my body heal itself so I can share that knowledge with others.

Now that I'm getting older perhaps I should more regularly ask God to fulfill His promise in Psalm 121:3 NIV *He will not let your foot slip--he who watches over you will not slumber;*

Scripture Kiss:

God's healing touch coupled with the advice of professionals.

Many a man has failed because he had his wishbone where his backbone should have been.

—Ronald Reagan

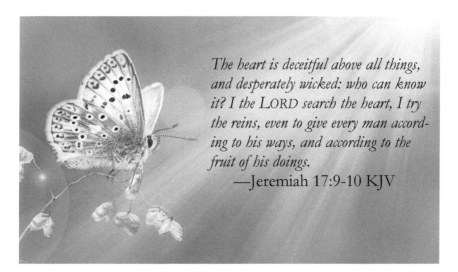

The heart is deceitful above all things, and desperately wicked: who can know it? I the LORD search the heart, I try the reins, even to give every man according to his ways, and according to the fruit of his doings.
—Jeremiah 17:9-10 KJV

Infected Thumb

I can remember when my son came to me complaining about pain in his thumb. It appeared he had an abscess filled with infection. I suggested it be lanced so it could begin the healing process. He differed in his opinion. Since he was over 18 and responsible for his own decisions, he waited. Two days later things looked pretty serious. Fortunately, a doctor from church saw it and insisted that my son come to his home so he could take care of his infected thumb.

It was so bad our friend had to dig very deep to find the core cause. A large pus pocket was beginning to congeal. How much pain and discomfort my son could have been spared if he had tended to the problem when it first manifested itself. (Isn't it interesting that our children and spouses are so slow to take our advice until forced by a doctor?)

We sometimes do that same thing with sin. We don't want the discomfort of giving up something that is poisoning our body or mind. We decide not to deal with it. The next thing we know the infectious sin has spread and is causing radiating pain and discomfort to us and those closest to us. We need to visit the Master Physician and let Him perform whatever surgery is needed so the healing process can begin.

With Kisses From Heaven

The command found in Luke 21:36, to *Watch therefore, and pray always that you may be counted worthy to escape all these things that will come to pass, and to stand before the Son of Man."* is also a promise. To watch and pray will be the duty of every Christian until Jesus returns. With total confidence we can feel secure in the truth that God never asks us to do anything that He is not willing to help us do. When we call out for strength to resist temptation our prayers are immediately answered, but we are expected to remove ourselves from the cause of temptation. The devil has no power over one that remains humbly in prayer before the Lord.

It is easier to resist temptation than to live with the consequences.

No temptation has overtaken you except such as is common to man; but God is faithful, who will not allow you to be tempted beyond what you are able, but with the temptation will also make the way of escape, that you may be able to bear it.—1 Corinthians 10:13.

Sometimes we are unaware that we are living in sin or have developed sinful habits.

To prevent living with this 'blind spot' in our life, it would be well for us to echo the prayer that David prayed in Psalm 139:23-24, 19:12, *Search me, O God and know my heart; Try me, and know my anxieties; and see if* there is any *wicked way in me, and lead me in the way everlasting. Who can understand* his *errors? Cleanse me from secret* faults. God's repeated warnings are clearly stated, as in Psalm 66:18: *If I regard iniquity in my heart, the Lord will not hear.*

Scripture Kisses:

I am convicted of the importance of keeping things right with God, not burying anything in our heart or in our life that can fester and cause more serious problems later.

We are reminded not to compromise with sin. Deal with it immediately.

But do not forget to do good and to share, for with such sacrifices God is well pleased.—Hebrews 13:16

Laborers Of Love

As a manager, I worked long hours and my schedule was full. It was never a typical eight-hour day. I came and went according to needs at the hospital, particularly the demands of the Emergency Room.

As I walked around the house that weekend, I became aware of the repairs that had been neglected and that needed to be made on the house. All of the work seemed overwhelming for one person. Remembering God's promise to provide for my needs, I began to pray to Him as my husband, to please work things out and get the repairs done before more damage occurred. Then I waited.

I met many wonderful people who interviewed to be on my volunteer chaplaincy team. My very special team grew to be family to one another. We generally learned a lot about each other through the 12-week training process. By the end of that time we were pretty tight. We had an understanding of each other's past struggles, present challenges, and heart's desire to serve the Lord with the gifts and talents He had entrusted to us.

One evening after we had shared some of our personal concerns with one another, one of my volunteers suggested that I might put out an invitation to the team for help with my home repair needs. My back deck was disintegrating and was badly in need of replacement. He suggested that we could plan a workday followed by a BBQ, which I would provide in appreciation, and then they could take a swim in the pool and/or play some outdoor games. That sounded like a pretty good idea to me, and those standing around listening gave resounding approval.

One of my volunteers lived on a religious compound where they follow both Jesus and their guru. One of the spiritual leaders there was also a contractor and a dear friend of mine. My volunteer decided to talk to his leader and share my needs.

When they heard that the back deck was old and rotting, becoming somewhat of a hazard, they got a work crew together. If I had the materials there, they would replace my back deck and build a new one.

True to their word, the scheduled workday arrived and so did a crew of carpenters ready for action. By the end of the day there was a transformation because of my "laborers of love." God allowed me the gift of these friends to bless His home and get things in order.

The concern and love that flowed from this workgroup was a testimony to me. They were kindhearted, gentle in spirit, caring and generous, just how I picture the Lord. Jesus instructed in John 13:34-35 *A new commandment I give to you, that you love one another; as I have loved you, that you also love one another. By this all will know that you are My disciples, if you have love for one another.* We are to live our life in such a way that others will be drawn to Him. Oh that we all might exemplify Christ's character with such intention.

Ye have not chosen me, but I have chosen you, and ordained you, that ye should go and bring forth fruit, and that your fruit should remain: that whatsoever ye shall ask of the Father in my name, he may give it you.
—John 15:16 KJV.

Love begets love. Friendship begets friendship. I once heard the saying, If you want to make a friend, ask them for help. Today I was gifted with a number of new friends.

When we reach out in Jesus' name desirous of sharing His love, we produce fruit. The fruit produced here was reciprocated by this team sacrificing and sharing their love, and blessing me in return.

I also knew the Lord promises in Isaiah 54:4-10 to be my Husband—One Who would care for me and provide for all my needs and He came through again. He is a Husband Who never fails and can always be trusted.

The day gained me new friends and a new deck!

Scripture Kisses:

The Lord as my husband takes care of all my needs as they arise by choosing others with a willing heart who can also benefit from what I have to offer.

Love begets love.

 Butterfly Kiss:

Love is like a butterfly: It goes where it pleases and it pleases wherever it goes.

—Author unknown

Be thankful in all circumstances, for this is God's will for you who belong to Christ Jesus.—1 Thessalonians 5:18 NLT.

Take comfort in God's promise that He watches over you and He wants to give you victory.

—Henry Blackaby, *Experiencing God,* p224

Pride goeth before destruction, and an haughty spirit before a fall.
—Proverbs 16:18 KJV.

Lemon Meringue Pie

This building project was going to take a while. The most productive use of our time and finances would be to live on the property while building our house.

The temperature was dropping rapidly. Living in a garage that had only been framed and covered with the outside wood sheeting didn't seem too promising or hold out much hope for a warm winter.

Five sons and number six on the way, all in a two-car garage? Hmmm? People in third-world countries surely got by with less. We could do it, I thought.

With as much creativity as I could muster, I visually, then physically, divided the garage into sections. Boys' bedroom area here, living room and kitchen area across the middle. Dad and Mom's sleeping area on this end with space saved for our new baby. All arranged! A small trailer parked outside the garage door provided bathroom and shower accommodations.

The next day it snowed. My husband showed up with a very old and rusted wood stove and ran the flue through the outside wall. The next morning creosote had dripped all over the living room furniture. We needed to reassess our situation.

With Kisses From Heaven

Cooking for seven and getting kids off to school was slow going. We had a lot of settling-in to do.

Then my husband made me a deal. "You're known for your prize-winning lemon meringue pies. We all love your pies and we haven't had one in a long time. I will get you that beautiful wood stove we looked at and install it in the garage to keep us warm and for you to cook on, on one condition. You have to promise, the first thing you make on the stove is a lemon meringue pie. Is it a deal?"

I said, "You've got to be kidding!" I was pretty proud of my reputation and I didn't want to ruin it by failing. My first reaction was, 'I don't know if I can do it on a wood stove. I've had to go from a gas stove to learning an electric stove, now a camping stove to a wood stove. But I decided, okay. I'm willing to try. Not everybody had to know about it if it were a failure.

So he got us a beautiful cook stove for the garage. A few days later this lovely new woodburning cook stove was delivered and installed in our garage abode. As promised, I went right to work as soon as it was ready. I washed it down and started working on my lemon pie, everything from scratch. I was eager to make the promised pie so I could begin using the stove to make meals for the family.

I decided to use my extra large glass pie plate. I made the crust and stuck it in the oven. It came out nice and flaky. I set it aside. Sometimes lemons are tangy and sweet, other times they don't have much flavor. These lemons were especially good. We were off to a good start!

I put the first ingredients for the filling in a pan on the stove to thicken. This was fun. It worked great. I was keeping careful watch, stirring constantly and moving the pan from one spot to another on the surface of the wood stove so it wouldn't burn. I could slide it from a cooler spot back to a warmer spot when I was ready. I was really enjoying this. Things were moving right along. So far, so good.

Lemon Meringue Pie

The lemons were perfect. The filling tasted wonderful. This is really good! I thought to myself. Now what about the meringue? I piled it on.

It looked good, but was it going to burn in the oven? I had some concern. I kept peeking to see how it was doing. I couldn't believe my eyes. It was browning slightly and evenly. This is what wood heat does? Wow! It was perfect, evenly golden all over the top. I had never made a pie so beautiful. I was so excited. 'This is the best lemon meringue pie I've ever made' I boosted to myself. I can't wait until the family sees this one. My husband will be surprised. 'Ha ha, he wasn't so sure I could do it,' I smirked.

Time to take it out. I waited until just the right moment. I reached for the potholders, opened the oven, and pulled out the shelf to remove this prize-winning pie. I couldn't wait to show this one off!!! I couldn't wait to serve it after supper.

To my horror, there was no stop on the shelf. Within all of two seconds my most prized beautiful lemon meringue pie went 'splat' all over the cement floor of our garage home. I was crushed. The pie plate broke so there was glass throughout everything.

That fast, my best pie was only a memory in my mind. The family didn't even get to see it. Now no one would ever see the most beautiful pie I had ever made or tasted. My husband wouldn't be able to taste it, but at least I had kept my word and baked it.

That night when I told my story in anguish, bemoaning my earlier experience with bitter disappointment, my young son shook his head and said, "Well Mom, you know what you always tell us, *pride goeth before a fall.* You always remind us the Bible says that." I couldn't argue with Proverbs 16:18 KJV!

Father, please forgive me for being so prideful and haughty. Help me walk in humility.

With Kisses From Heaven

We know God hates pride. It also reminded me of the saying, Pride is the only disease that makes everyone sick but the one who has it.—Buddy Robinson. I'd like to keep people from feeling sick after they have been with me and help their day be better because of an encounter with me.

Scripture Kiss:

God lovingly reveals when we have a pride issue and will help purge it from our life.

"Judge not, that you be not judged.
—Matthew 7:1

Locked Door

I was so excited. That extra 20 pounds I had put on had finally disappeared. I had some cute clothes that were now too large. I thought it might be worth it financially to have them altered. I started checking around for someone who might be able to help me. I got a lead on a gal who attended our church.

I gave her a call and was so glad to find she would be available. I gathered my clothes together, loaded them in the car and headed to her house.

When I arrived, I scooped up a pile of clothes. With my arms full, I finally was able to ring the doorbell. The door had small windows in it. I looked inside but didn't see anyone coming. I could hear noise inside but there was no response. I rang the bell again and waited ... and waited. I was just about to ring the bell once more and knock loudly when the seamstress showed up. I heard keys rattling, then one at a time she unlocked three locks on the door. I was astonished—three key locks!?

While we were busy going through the clothes, her small children were running and playing around us. I completed giving instructions for each item. We made an appointment for my next visit and I left.

During the next few weeks, I revisited, in my mind, my encounter with this lady and her family. I couldn't believe that she had three key locks on her front door!

As I was headed to her home to pick up the items she had altered for me, I again remembered my previous visit. I began to pray for her. My prayer was conversational. I said something like, "Father, this poor lady. Three locks on her door. She must live in terrible fear. I come against the enemy of fear and pray peace and safety over her, over her family. Father please set her free from this paralyzing fear and any repercussion that would fall upon her children."

To my surprise God began speaking to my heart. "Derry, you have assumed and passed judgment on her. Did you notice that she lives in a corner house on busy roads? She has two small children. Her son is very rambunctious and is hard to contain. He can open the door. She locks the door so her children won't go outside without her knowledge and end up in traffic. She is not living in fear."

Ouch, I had misjudged her and her locked doors. I thought my heart was compassionate and concerned. God showed me my heart was judgmental and I had jumped to conclusions. This encounter made me think of the scripture found in John 7:24, *Do not judge according to appearance, but judge with righteous judgment.* Things are not always as they appear!

Scripture Kiss:

God is all wise and all knowing. We are not. We should pray for others but not make assumptions or judgments.

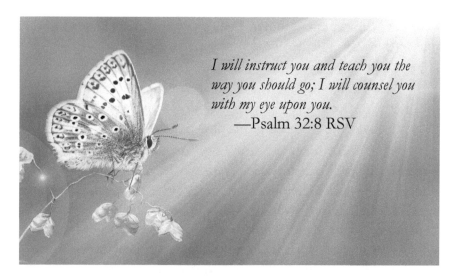

I will instruct you and teach you the way you should go; I will counsel you with my eye upon you.
—Psalm 32:8 RSV

Morning Line-Up

One of my sisters is ten years younger than me. I left for boarding school when she was only five. Most of her growing up years we were separated in distance. When I came home she knew I was her sister but I was still a stranger to her. We had always lived a long distance apart and never had opportunity to spend much time together, even after we married and began growing our families.

Holidays brought reunion and an opportunity for cousins to meet and play at Grandma and Grandpa's house; but those interactions were all too brief. I admired my sister, her wit, cheerfulness, creative abilities, intelligence and I thought she was adorable. As a child she had been the cutest cheerleader. Today she was just plain beautiful. I enjoyed being in her presence, just watching and listening to her prattle on in her very entertaining way.

I was thrilled when she asked me if I would let her daughter live with me for a while when she was moving and settling in. My niece was four years old, as adorable as her mother had been as a child and just as perky!

At the time she joined our family, we had six sons and one on the way. The boys were very excited that their cousin, a girl, would be coming to live with us.

We had expected them to arrive around dinner time but circumstances delayed their arrival. My sons went to bed knowing that in the morning our new resident would be there!

The next morning I was busy in the kitchen preparing breakfast. Usually the boys were down by now and hanging around the kitchen helping and observing, but today it was quiet. I wondered if everyone was upstairs visiting and welcoming my niece. Then I heard movement, but no conversation. I completed what I was doing at the stove, dried my hands, and headed the direction of the sound.

What I saw stunned me, but made me smile with amusement. At the request of my niece, six boys, ages three through 15, were obediently lined up on the hearth, sitting quietly with glazed eyes. She however had taken her stance centered about four feet out in the room. With her little finger wagging at them she was laying out the program for the day, giving each one their instructions. With puzzled faces and mouths agape they sat listening, eyes wide. No one moved.

When I came around the corner she smoothed her little dress and smiled. I just stood there with a grin on my face. I looked at the morning lineup and assured them, "Guys … you don't have to do what she says." They took a deep breath and sighed in relief.

It was all quite amusing. Her presence in our home made me realize how inherently manipulative the female of the species can be. This "good-morning line-up" made me think of several scriptures with all different points to punctuate:

First, God wants to be the One to direct us. Psalm 32:8 RSV, *I will instruct you and teach you the way you should go; I will counsel you with my eye upon you.*

The next thing I hate to admit, but all my sons just obediently followed. No one questioned or challenged. That made me think we can be, as Isaiah 53:7 RSV says, *He was oppressed, and he was afflicted, yet he opened not his mouth; like a lamb that is led to the slaughter, and like a sheep that before its shearers is dumb, so he opened not his mouth.*

But lastly, on a more positive note, Isaiah 11:6 RSV, … *and a little child shall lead them.* Truly this little child was leading. She has a lot of leadership ability. We should never underestimate the power of a child. They can do much for the Kingdom of God if they know Him and are taught to walk in His way.

We have the opportunity of gaining knowledge and wisdom from many places, even from a child! We also have a responsibility to lead them in the "good way" and teach them about Jesus.

Scripture Kiss:

God wants to lead us and direct us. It is His voice we must recognize and acknowledge.

 Butterfly Kiss:

Le papillon est une fleur qui vole,

La fleur un papillon fixe.

[The butterfly is a flying flower,

The flower a tethered butterfly.]

—Ponce Denis Écouchard-Lebrun

Do nothing from selfishness or conceit, but in humility count others better than yourselves. Let each of you look not only to his own interests, but also to the interests of others.—Philippians 2:3-4 RSV.

Each individual is given the opportunity to help bring light to a world struggling to find its way in the swirl of darkness.

—Author unknown. 1992 Prayer Journal, Birth.

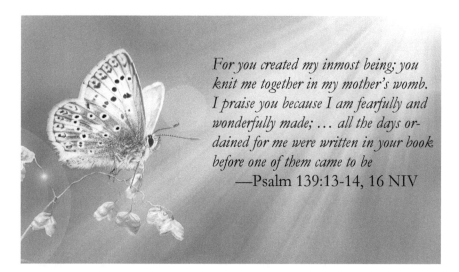

For you created my inmost being; you knit me together in my mother's womb. I praise you because I am fearfully and wonderfully made; ... all the days ordained for me were written in your book before one of them came to be
—Psalm 139:13-14, 16 NIV

Pizza Buffet

One evening my husband decided he wanted to go to a pizza buffet for dinner. When we got there, there was only one parking place left. There was a line of people inside and down the front of the building waiting to get in.

I went to the front of the line to put our name on the waiting list. When I got there the young lady taking names said, "Just a minute. I will be right back." I stepped to the side. She headed for the cash register and remained there for some time. The place was really hopping. She alone was quite busy. After she finished at the cash register she grabbed a cloth and started wiping down tables, then back to the cash register. The pizza buffet was obviously short-handed. I came forward again to get our names on the waiting list. I was at the head of the second line.

I stood watching. I could count five empty tables. No one had time to clear them so others could be seated. The line would have thinned more quickly if only the people could be seated. However the line was still so long, it was going to take a while for everyone to be served. Most tables seated at least four. Most people in line were there as a couple.

With Kisses From Heaven

A lady came up beside me to put her name on the list. Both of us were waiting for our husbands to find us in line. She had the same problem I had. No one was there to take her name.

Therefore receive one another, just as Christ also received us, to the glory of God.—Romans 15:7.

We chatted for a while observing the situation together and then I said, "There are so many people waiting. I wouldn't mind sharing a table if you like." Then I introduced myself. "By the way, my name is Derry."

She just looked at me. "What did you say your name is?"

"Derry."

"That's crazy. My name is Daria."

About then both our husbands came up to find out what was going on. We introduced them and guess what? They were both Ron.

At that moment the verse in Isaiah 49:16 NLT came to mind, *See, I have written your name on the palms of my hands.* ... It reminded me that no matter what our name is, or how many people have the same name as us, we are all special in God's eyes. He knows us individually and has a divine plan for each person. He knows everything about us. He is mindful of everything that concerns us and He will see us through. When we show each other acceptance we are being what He calls us to be—His disciples.

Scripture Kiss:

We are each precious to Jesus. He knows us by name.

But I fear, lest somehow, as the serpent deceived Eve by his craftiness, so your minds may be corrupted from the simplicity that is in Christ.
—2 Corinthians 11:3

Snake On The Table

The boys were outside playing. They were being very understanding of me isolating in order to have papers ready for the deadline. It was tax time. I was gathering all of the necessary paperwork and information so we could complete what was needed to give to the accountant.

I had been laboring on this project for several days. The dining room table was taken over with piles of papers sorted into appropriate sections to accommodate what we would be reporting. I was completely absorbed in this project and eager to get it off my plate.

I was so intent that I only barely noticed the boys entering through the front door. I had my adding machine out and I was hard at it. Then out of the corner of my eye I caught something flying through the air. I looked up just in time to see a snake land on the table right in front of me. A snake on the table!!!

I did exactly what you would expect—and what they were hoping for: I jumped up and out of my chair with a scream! That of course delighted my sons who had launched the wicked serpent my direction. They were giggling with delight. I hollered, "Get this thing out of here!" Barely able to contain themselves they quickly removed it. Talk about a memory ... this story is still repeated to our grandchildren.

As I was sharing this story recently, so many spiritual lessons came to mind, like how the enemy, the devil, satan, catches us off guard. He sneaks up on us and tries to tempt us and deceive us. James 1:13-14 tells us, *Let no one say when he is tempted, "I am tempted by God"; for God cannot be tempted by evil, nor does He Himself tempt anyone. But each one is tempted when he is drawn away by his own desires and enticed.*

We are instructed in Luke 22:40 *When He came to the place, He said to them, "Pray that you may not enter into temptation."*

Jesus died on the cross, and on that cross the devil, satan was defeated and disarmed. We can now walk in His victory. Luke 10:17-20 says, *Then the seventy returned with joy, saying, "Lord, even the demons are subject to us in Your name." And He said to them, "I saw Satan fall like lightning from heaven. Behold, I give you the authority to trample on serpents and scorpions, and over all the power of the enemy, and nothing shall by any means hurt you. Nevertheless do not rejoice in this, that the spirits are subject to you, but rather rejoice because your names are written in heaven.*

Jesus went through the whole cross experience to defeat him and give us a hope for our future. And at the end of life here on earth, Revelation 20:2-3 tells us what will happen to him, *He laid hold of the dragon, that serpent of old, who is the Devil and Satan, and bound him for a thousand years; and he cast him into the bottomless pit, and shut him up, and set a seal on him, so that he should deceive the nations no more till the thousand years were finished. But after these things he must be released for a little while.*

Our prayer to our Father is for Him to fulfill the promise in Matthew 6:13, *And do not lead us into temptation, But deliver us from the evil one. For Yours is the kingdom and the power and the glory forever. Amen.* Then we are assured in 1 Corinthians 10:13 that, *No temptation has overtaken you except such as is common to man; but God is faithful, who will not allow you to be tempted beyond what you are able, but with the temptation will also make the way of escape, that you may be able to bear* it. We are to stand firm. Once we have endured we can depend upon the scripture promise in Luke 4:13, *Now when the devil had ended every temptation, he departed from Him until an opportune time.*

When we are distracted and unaware, the enemy sneaks in, catching us off guard and tries to snatch us out of God's hands, but we must stand firm against the devil. When Jesus was tempted by the devil His response was, "It is written." The Word of God was His weapon and it is ours as well.

Scripture Kiss:

When the enemy sneaks up on us, we have God to turn to and He will save us.

 Butterfly Kiss:

Just as God creates new life for the caterpillar, changing its very DNA, and transforming it into a butterfly; so God transforms us into a new creation with new beginnings.

Faithful are the wounds of a friend, But deceitful are the kisses of an enemy.—Proverbs 27:6 NASB.

The joy of life is made up of obscure and seemingly mundane victories that give us our own small satisfactions.

—Billy Joel

There are "friends" who destroy each other, but a real friend sticks closer than a brother.—Proverbs 18:24 NLT

Spaghetti Disaster

One of my first jobs was as administrative secretary to the Vice President of Installment Loans at a large city bank. While working there I met some friends who have become lifelong buddies. One in particular is Marilyn. She was the administrative secretary for the Vice President of International Affairs.

At the time we met, I was recently married and she was about to be married. I loved to cook and Marilyn was learning. We had a few "sessions" together to help her feel more secure for her new role as wife. She was a fast learner.

We enjoyed each other as couples and often arranged time to be together. We applauded each other's successes and were there for each other through the challenges of young couples growing our families.

Marilyn was the first to get pregnant. My pregnancy was about a year behind hers. In fact I was pregnant with my first when she was pregnant with her second child. We had become best friends. When we were together there was generally a lot of laughter. We also learned pregnant women can become a bit emotional and even impatient sometimes. We were sensitive to each other's moods.

With Kisses From Heaven

Because we were still "newlyweds" and projecting plans for the future, we were excited for each other when we started hunting to purchase our first home. Saving for a deposit on a home means you bite the bullet and become very frugal. We were all used to that and we did it together. Back in those days we could stretch a can of tuna and extend it enough for all of us to enjoy a sandwich together. We were able to do that later with our children, too!

We were the first to get into a new home. We were so excited. The first people we wanted to host there were our dear friends Bob and Marilyn. They had a toddler and we had a carpeted dining room. I wasn't thinking. Getting into the house had taken all of our finances, so we were back to eating as inexpensively as possible. That meant spaghetti!

Our friends arrived, highchair in hand. I had a beautifully set table. I couldn't wait to show Marilyn the house. After the tour we were off to the kitchen together. Seemed our moods are a bit on edge. She chased her son. I get the food served. She placed him in the highchair. We had the blessing. She put spaghetti on his tray. He dropped spaghetti on the carpet. I picked up the spaghetti and wiped up the carpet. He threw more spaghetti down before I could think of putting something under his highchair to protect the carpet. I cleaned it up and sat back down to "enjoy" my meal. By now the baby had been indulging in the very greasy garlic bread, seemingly enjoying it. Then he threw it on the carpet. I got up and grabbed it off the carpet and clean the carpet again. I sat back down.

Marilyn and I are both getting frustrated by now. The baby started wiggling in his chair wanting to get out. Marilyn picked him up and set him down on the carpet—garlic oil all over his hands. I can't hold it back any longer. I say, "Marilyn, really? My new home!"

To my shock she jumped up and said, "That's enough. Bob, we're going home—now!" I tried to backpedal but to no avail. They left and I sat there choking down the rest of my dinner through tears.

I was crushed. Why hadn't I thought about covering the carpet? Why hadn't I handled this differently? I had hurt and offended my dearest friend.

As I lay awake in bed that night revisiting the evening, I vowed that never again would anything I owned become more important than a person. I vowed to make my home a place where all were welcome and nothing became so sacred that I would be on pins and needles to protect it.

The next morning I called my dear friend and apologized. She in turn apologized to me. We both agreed, perhaps our fragile emotions stemmed from our pregnancies. We confirmed our commitment of friendship and sisterhood. Since our spaghetti disaster, now over 50 years later, we are still giggling over the phone and keeping track of one another though we live thousands of miles apart. Our phone calls usually include an invitation to come over for a tuna sandwich.

Not only have I been blessed with some very precious friends but I have found that Jesus is a Friend Who never lets us down. As I write these words, I am reminded of the story in scripture of King Hezekiah who despite popular opinion chose to follow God and God blessed him. In times when it isn't popular to follow God, when the forces of evil are attempting to blot out His name and deny His Kingship, it takes courage to take a stand for our Creator God—God of love.

If you want to prosper in life, seek the will and way of Jesus—a true and proven Friend—the Friend Who is always by our side.

Do not judge, and you will not be judged. Do not condemn, and you will not be condemned. Forgive, and you will be forgiven.—Luke 6:37 NIV.

With Kisses From Heaven

Scripture Kiss:

God's forgiveness, reconciliation and friendship are offered to each of us:

In all this I have given you an example that by such work we must support the weak, remembering the words of the Lord Jesus, for he himself said, 'It is more blessed to give than to receive.'"—Acts 20:35 NRSV.

To receive a present handsomely and in a right spirit, even when you have none to give in return, is to give one in return.

—Leigh Hunt

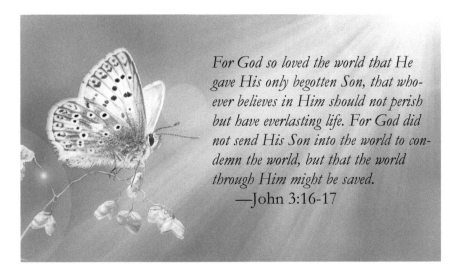

For God so loved the world that He gave His only begotten Son, that whoever believes in Him should not perish but have everlasting life. For God did not send His Son into the world to condemn the world, but that the world through Him might be saved.
—John 3:16-17

Spring Baskets

Christian churches refer to Easter Sunday as Resurrection Sunday. This noteworthy day and Passover generally come around springtime—a time of new beginnings. We focus on our Lord and we focus on His children. We use this day the world celebrates as Easter as an opportunity to share Jesus.

To keep it fun for the children I would hide several baskets. One basket was full of small loaves of bread, wrapped in colored cellophane, tied with a bow holding a short shock of wheat. Another basket held some bouquets of flowers tied with ribbon. Another held children's coloring books about the resurrection rolled with a ribbon and a small box of crayons. There was also a basket that held home-crafted refrigerator magnets with scriptures on them.

The children had to go on a treasure hunt in order to locate the baskets. When they were all retrieved we would head off to visit a neighborhood. We would knock at the door and say "Happy Spring, we brought you some gifts." Each boy would come forward with his gift. We would ask if they had children and if so they would each get a coloring book. They were then offered the basket with magnets and invited to choose the one they wanted.

With Kisses From Heaven

Jesus says in Matthew 28:19, *Go therefore and make disciples of all the nations.* We have all been invited and called to be His disciples. Our sons learned early in their life that we can all plant seeds for Jesus just by sharing. We can all do our part. Sometimes it just takes a little creativity—like spring baskets.

God so loved the world ... and He called us to share the news.

The thief does not come except to steal, and to kill, and to destroy. I have come that they may have life, and that they may have it more abundantly.—John 10:10. Let's share that good news with the world around us.

Scripture Kiss:

God called us to share the good news.—He loves us!

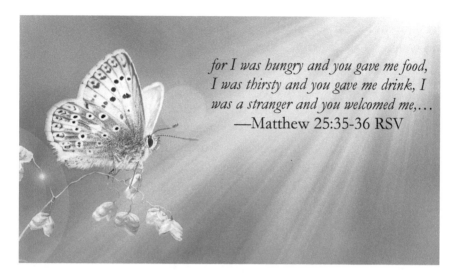

for I was hungry and you gave me food, I was thirsty and you gave me drink, I was a stranger and you welcomed me,...
—Matthew 25:35-36 RSV

Surprise Package

My family was transitioning after my dad's death. I was the oldest of five children, four girls and the youngest a boy. Mom had to look for work and we had to figure out how to make ends meet.

I had been looking forward to going to college but now that looked uncertain. I made a few phone calls and spoke to the financial advisor at the college to see if there would be extra work available for me there. After lining up three jobs at the college, including summer work, my hopes were up.

I sat down and talked it over with Mom. I promised her I wouldn't ask her for any financial help and pointed out that my absence could save her some on the food bill and expenses of my personal necessities. My arguments seemed reasonable to her so she agreed.

I knew it was going to take superhuman strength to pull this off. I also knew God was on my side and would enable me to do the work and help me handle my studies.

My summer schedule had me up by 4am every morning for the first shift at the cafeteria. I then went back to the dorm and changed. The next job was outside for yard maintenance, about an hour of free time, then back to the cafeteria to help prepare and serve supper, then back to the girls' dorm to work the welcome desk until 10pm.

It was working at the cafeteria where I met many new friends, both those working there and those coming through the line regularly. One particular gentleman comes to mind. He stood out because of his circumstances. He was older than almost all the students, probably somewhere in his early 30s. He was from Denmark. He continually showed up just after the cafeteria closed, looking worn and disheveled. I wasn't sure if he had just awakened from a nap or had just run a marathon!

In any event, as a server, I had my area to clean up. It was my responsibility to put away any leftover food and get the serving trays over to the dishwasher. Inevitably, Erling would show up right after I had put the food away and cleared my area. He would come, in a panic, eyes wide, looking around. Then he would sigh and taking his hand push his hair back off of his face as he shook his head as if to say "Oh no!" I was reminded by my supervisor that the line was closed and I could not serve him. She told me he would have to learn to get there on time. He would hang his head and walk out the door. I can't remember ever seeing anyone speak to him, welcome him or ask him why he had trouble getting there on time. That troubled me.

The third time it happened, I was ready for him. Before everyone put their food away, I served him out a plate of food and put it in the warmer. Just as before he rushed in, looked around, sighed, hung his head and started out the door. This time I called to him. He turned and looked at me.

I said, "You seem to be having a little trouble getting here in time for supper. I have something for you. I hope I made the right food choices for you." I handed him the plate.

I thought he was going to cry. With moist eyes he bowed his head and thanking me, took the plate of food and retreated to a table alone.

I hadn't eaten yet so I took my plate of food and asked if I could join him. He seemed happy for the company. That was when I learned a number of things about him. He was also keeping a grueling schedule and often fell asleep sometime in the late afternoon just prior to supper. Other times, since his job was a distance from the cafeteria, even when he hurried he had trouble making it on time. I encouraged him, then advised, "you really need to show up here at least five minutes earlier." I asked him if he thought he could do that. I told him if he would make an effort to get there before the cafeteria closed, I would make him a plate of food occasionally if he didn't make it. I think he was only late once after that, several weeks later. Now he was also coming cleaned up, hair combed and shaven.

Life makes a difference when we have someone in our corner; someone who expresses concern and interest and is willing to encourage us on. That's what happened with Erling.

I witnessed an amazing change in him. He was so grateful for this small act of kindness. We became good friends and encouraged each other along.

When I left college the following summer my college roommate and I took a room together in a hospital-owned apartment building and both got jobs at the hospital. When we first started working there, finances hadn't been enough to cover our current obligations. We had a couple of nights where we were digging through old purses looking for change in hopes of finding some grocery money.

One week when we were really struggling we were surprised to get a notice that we needed to go down to the train station to retrieve a parcel. Confused about what it might be, we found a friend with a vehicle and made our way there. Somehow Erling found out about our plight. I don't know how, but his timing was perfect. I'm guessing God had something to do with it because we had been praying for help. He sent me a surprise package—a huge box filled with all kinds of food and some encouraging gifts of thanks for all I had done for him that school year.

I remember when I was young, there was an old saying, "One good turn deserves another."

That certainly happened with me and my new friend Erling. We each had an opportunity to bless one another and fill God's word in Ephesians 4:32 RSV, *and be kind to one another, tenderhearted, ….* And in Luke 6:31 *And just as you want men to do to you, you also do to them likewise.*

Scripture Kiss:

The blessing of friendship can come from acts of kindness.

 Butterfly Kiss:

God's blessings are sometimes like butterfly kisses; you can't feel them because they are so soft and loving.

—Dorothy Matthews

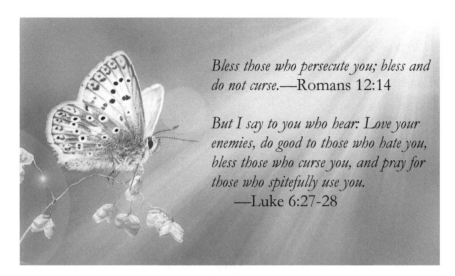

Bless those who persecute you; bless and do not curse.—Romans 12:14

But I say to you who hear: Love your enemies, do good to those who hate you, bless those who curse you, and pray for those who spitefully use you.
—Luke 6:27-28

The Unoffendable Christ

I recently attended a conference that left a life-changing impact on me. It consisted of parallel themes. One was "The Unoffendable Christ". The other was, "Bless Your Enemies."

A frequent prayer of mine is, "Father, help me be more like Jesus." I don't present a list of Jesus character qualities to God with that prayer. I simply ask to be like Jesus. As I listened to the speaker talk about the "Unoffendable Christ" I thought, that's how I want to be. If we truly want to follow Christ's example, we will take note of His instruction given in the above texts. I prayed right then that God would help me follow Jesus' example and live without taking, carrying or giving offense.

Next, I listened to the speaker share how Jesus instructed us to bless those who persecute and despitefully treat us. I had read these verses before but the full impact of the words had never really penetrated. I looked up the texts in the Bible. Sure enough, there it was in **red** letters—Jesus' words. Jesus is asking for action. We are to **do** what the text tells us to do.

It was King David who wanted to destroy his enemies and called upon God to punish them—get even. But Jesus' counsel is to bless and pray for our enemies. I read through the text again and allowed the Holy Spirit to quicken my mind as to what was being taught. I prayed a heartfelt commitment to apply this instruction; these two themes to my life. This resolve was soon tested.

I had a five-hour ride home that enabled me to contemplate and saturate myself in this teaching. I was working through how I actually apply this in my life.

When I finally arrived I was tired, hungry and eager to unpack and prepare for the new week. One of my sons had temporarily moved back home. I entered the house, greeting those present. Not having had a good day, my son greeted me with less than respect. As a matter of fact his response was downright rude.

My unspoken thought was, "whatever is wrong with him?" Disgruntled by his greeting I carried my things on down to my room. I set my suitcases down thinking, "What is his problem anyway? He moved back in here with me. This is my little sanctuary. My safe place. I don't need to come home and deal with an attitude ..."

Ooops, I suddenly remembered, "the Unoffendable Christ, blessed." Luke 6:27-28, *But I say to you who hear: Love your enemies, do good to those who hate you, bless those who curse you, and pray for those who spitefully use you.* And David prays in Psalm 19:14, *Let the words of my mouth and the meditations of my heart Be acceptable in Your sight, O LORD my strength and my Redeemer.*

I went to my office and began praying. "Father, please bless my son. Please bless him with respect and honor for his parents. Bless him with the desire for relationship and unity; with unconditional love and repentance. Please bless him with the gift of communication, a desire for reconciliation, and a cheerful spirit; with the knowledge that You are the parent that is always there for him even when he feels that his earthly parents have failed him."

It was only a few minutes later when he stormed up the office stairway to confront me. I had already applied my "secret weapon." I could not be moved. He muttered a few words. They didn't affect me. They were like water off a duck's back. I responded gently. Peace prevailed and I celebrated victory.

I have been crucified with Christ, it is no longer I who live, but Christ lives in me; and the life *which I now live in the flesh I live by faith in the Son of God, who loved me and gave Himself for me.*—Galatians 2:20.

Is there someone in your life who needs a blessing and prayer-covering today? Is there someone you need to forgive?

This scripture lesson has been lived out in my life repeatedly. God's word is true. When we bless and pray for our enemies, or those that offend us, as He directs us, then God can move in and take care of things. If we hold grudges and build up resentment and bitterness, it is rather like God stands aside with His arms folded saying, "Okay Derry, if you want to handle this, go ahead. When you are ready for me to step in, let me know."

Scripture Kiss:

When we do things God's way it always turns out best.

He who cannot forgive breaks the bridge over which he himself must pass.
—George Herbert

To forgive is to set a prisoner free and discover that the prisoner was you.
—Lewis B. Smedes

Whatever your hand finds to do, do it *with your might;* ...
　—Ecclesiastes 9:10.

The anointing of the heart by the Holy Spirit results in extraordinary power, wisdom and love. The anointing of the Holy Spirit enables confidence, courage and conviction ... blessed, filled and empowered by the Spirit of God.

　—Lloyd Ogilvie, *God's Best for My Life,*
　　August 3

Blessed is the one who perseveres under trial because, having stood the test, that person will receive the crown of life that the Lord has promised to those who love him.—James 1:12 NIV

The Wasp Stole Our Lunch

Usually we all went to town together. This time mother had to do some shopping with my sister for school clothes. Since my two-year-old baby sister was cutting teeth and not feeling well Mom asked if I would be willing to stay home with her.

Debbie was sleeping a lot and I had a book I was eager to finish reading. It sounded like a good plan. Mom trusted my abilities and wisdom. I was ten but quite capable...so I thought.

Debbie slept. I read. Poor baby was worn out from all the pain and discomfort. I checked the time. I thought I'd better get some lunch prepared so when she woke up I had everything ready. I headed for the kitchen. It had a swinging door. I walked in, screamed and walked out. I pushed the door open and peeked inside.

The kitchen had been taken over by a wasp ... an apparently very angry wasp! It was buzzing and flying fast back and forth across the kitchen, hitting into the two windows and swirling around. Still young and having experienced a wasp sting previously, I was very afraid of that wasp!

With Kisses From Heaven

I kept peeking in carefully, because that nasty wasp was covering the whole kitchen in flight—clear to the door where I was trying to get in. I was trying to figure out how I could get in there and make our lunch. It didn't seem like there was any safe way to do that. I was stuck…and hungry.

Off in the distance I heard a little voice, calling to get out of her crib. Oh no, Debbie was awake and would be hungry. This wasn't good. I could only hope Mom would be home soon to save the day.

I snuggled Debbie into my arms and rocked her, stroking her precious little curls, soothing her with a song. I was trying to put off the inevitable. My stall tactics didn't work for long. Just as I had suspected she was hungry. She also had a little fever.

I put her down on the sofa and headed to the kitchen to check out the situation. I was hoping the wasp had worn itself out. No such luck. I couldn't go in there. What was I going to do? Debbie was crying now. She wanted to eat. I was really hungry too. When would Mom be back?

I picked Debbie up and started walking around with her, looking out windows, pointing out flowers. She wiped her eyes and said, "Mommy. I want Mommy" I was becoming anxious. I didn't know what to do. I was afraid of the wasp and concerned about Mom's reaction when she got home and found out I hadn't fed Debbie.

As soon as Mom walked in the door she could hear Debbie crying, now almost wailing. She came in and took her out of my arms and asked what was wrong.

I didn't have to tell her … Debbie did. "Eat. Eat. Eat Please."

Mother turned around and looked at me. "Haven't you eaten lunch? Haven't you fed her anything?"

"No … I …."

"What have you been doing, young lady? I left you home, trusting you to take care of your little sister and you haven't even fed her?! What in the world happened to you?"

"Mom, I couldn't. There's a wasp in the kitchen and I couldn't go in."

"Did it occur to you that you could have snuck in and grabbed something out of the refrigerator and cupboards so you could make her a sandwich in another room? I'm so disappointed, Derry Lee. I trusted you and you really let me down ... and your little sister has suffered at your irresponsibility."

As far as I was concerned, that wasp had stolen our lunch. Broken-hearted and ashamed I made lunch ... as soon as Mom got the fly swatter and took care of the wasp. I learned that when you have been given a trust and responsibility, you find a way to keep your word ... you come through.

God's Word is clear about His expectations to those that have been given a trust:

Now it is required that those who have been given a trust must prove faithful.—1 Corinthians 4:2 NIV.

Scripture Kiss:

A lesson learned that was life-changing and has stayed with me throughout life—fulfill the responsibilities entrusted to you in a timely fashion. If difficulties come up—face them and find a way.

His lord said to him, 'Well done, good and faithful servant; you have been faithful over a few things, I will make you ruler over many things. Enter into the joy of your lord.'—Matthew 25:23.

Divine love never stops caring, never stops being concerned, never stops praying and never gives up.

    —Author unknown. 1992 Prayer Journal,
       Love

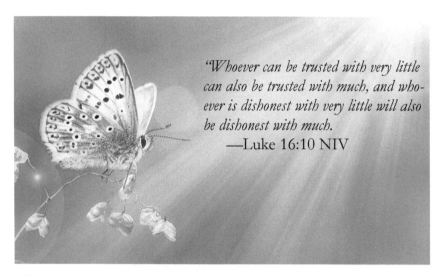

"Whoever can be trusted with very little can also be trusted with much, and whoever is dishonest with very little will also be dishonest with much.
—Luke 16:10 NIV

The Woodpecker Drained My Bank Account

There was a time many years ago when electric bills suddenly skyrocketed. Mine more than tripled!!! I was stunned to receive a bill for over $400. That seemed impossible so I did some investigating.

First I called the electric company. They gave me the meter report and assured me I had been billed accordingly. They asked me a series of questions to ascertain if I had excessive usage any where in the house. They particularly asked me about our well, the pump, and information about filling the water tank up the hill.

I decided to go up to the water tank to see if the shut off valve was working. To my amazement, I discovered that a woodpecker had drilled a large hole in my water tank. The pump in the well was running continuously to keep the tank full. One small hole equaled about $300 a month for several months. That small leak made by the woodpecker quickly drained my bank account.

It reminded me of a thought penned by Coleman Cox: "Even the woodpecker owes his success to the fact that he uses his head and keeps pecking away until he finishes the job he starts."

With Kisses From Heaven

I remember reading a story years ago about children who collected enough pennies to lay a railroad track. One penny at a time equaled a treasure chest full enough to accomplish a lifetime contribution that blessed many communities.

Shortly after reading that story I took a Financial Stewardship class. During my study of one of the lessons, there were some words that caused me deep contemplation. I applied them to our hospital's financial picture and realized what a marked difference they would make if everyone employed there were to take them to heart. I quote, "Covenant not to steal a stamp or a photocopy or a paperclip or a long-distance telephone call or a penny from your employer, the government or anyone else. The people of God must be honest in even the smallest seemingly inconsequential matters."

Stewardship is one of the values that the hospital emphasized. Good stewardship is an attribute that can affect us in every station of life. Careful management of our personal possessions and means can often make a large difference in our financial picture at home.

At that time the hospital had 859 recorded employees. What if each employee were to "forget" and inadvertently take home two pens a month (equivalent of two boxes of pens a year), a few paperclips, made an occasional personal photocopy, or place an occasional long-distance call (even if it is to say "please call me right back because I don't want to make long distance calls from work"?) We knew there was a problem with not returning silverware to dietary. We were frequently reminded to make returns to the kitchen. I wonder what else we forgot to return.

In some places, these issues are taken very seriously. A bitter pill to swallow is that our "forgetting" is actually stealing. A friend of mine worked for the county in another area. If someone was seen outside of the county offices with one of their pens, they were fired. Another medical facility had a rule that no one from dietary could take home any food that was left over. If an employee was caught taking food, they were fired.

For point of discussion, let's say each employee occasionally "forgot" or wasted paper, or tissues or some other supply just by not being careful. Let's say each person had room to grow in this area and individually they cost the hospital about $5 a month. Imagine ... $51,540.00 of expenses a year would have unintentionally been added to the hospital budget! Pretty significant!!!

Cut that in half—What if it were only a pen, a paper-clip, and maybe a photocopy or two? What if it were only $2.50 a month? That still comes to $25,770.00 a year for unnecessary expenses—stolen money!

Ones' attitude might be, the hospital is big enough and brings in enough money to handle that. Or, we might think this whole idea is a bit nit picky. But is it really? We were all very blessed to have a job; to be able to work and to have the benefits that were offered to us. The more each person does to help the financial base of their employer, the more it will benefit everyone in the long run. Perhaps if we were all a little more aware of our contribution to loss and if we all helped rectify whatever is in our power to effect; it might also bless us with less of a budget cut. (Just a thought!)

It is easy to excuse ourselves, and it is honorable that the employer "forgives" our carelessness; but I can't help but wonder if carelessness in little things could establish habits that could make us careless with other things in life. Maybe it would be good character growth for us to do some heart searching and see if we translate a problem in this area to taking advantage of others that we work with as well.

I resolved to be more "religiously" respectful of my employers' supplies and what I either cost or saved our institution. What if we each made it a game to see what a difference practicing "Stewardship" and "Carefulness" would make?

With Kisses From Heaven

His lord said to him, 'Well done, good and faithful servant; you have been faithful over a few things, I will make you ruler over many things. Enter into the joy of your lord.'—Matthew 25:23 NKJV.

This scripture reminded me how important the "little things" are. Are you with me? I'm willing for someone to hold me accountable. Are you?

One little woodpecker, one single person, can make the difference for good or harm.

Have you cultivated the habit of carefulness in all things or are you a woodpecker?

Scripture Kiss:

Accountability in stewardship helps us attain a higher standard of awareness, gratitude and consideration. Remember the woodpecker!

"For you shall go out with joy, And be led out with peace; The mountains and the hills Shall break forth into singing before you, And all the trees of the field shall clap their hands.—Isaiah 55:12

Trees Clap And Praise

Never would I have guessed that I would see the fulfillment of this verse, but I did. I truly did.

I was driving through the majestic mountains north of Grass Valley in California on my way to a speaking appointment. I can think of no other word for the beauty around me than "awesome." As I was driving I had my sunroof open and my praise music on. I was worshipping God with all my heart. I was singing and praying and thanking Him for His goodness, for the amazing day that it was, and the glory of His creation.

Everything around me was still, as far as I could see ahead, until I noticed that just before, I mean just before me as I was driving through, it was as though the trees were swaying and clapping at the sounds of praise, It wasn't wind! It was as though they were opening a way before me. I know that seems incredible and I am at a loss for words to adequately explain what I saw with my eyes. The trees were clapping and praising with me. I only know that the moment I saw it, the above verse, Isaiah 55:12, came to mind and I knew the presence of the Lord was leading me along.

I couldn't help but praise more and rejoice at this spectacular display of nature rejoicing to God. I wonder how much more of that I would see if I praised God in utter abandonment more often…as I did that day. How many things do I miss by not being attentive to my Lord? How much more would He reveal if I lived my life in total surrender and at oneness with Him every day?

Blessed be the name of the Lord. Blessed be His Holy name. Blessed be the Creator of all the universe. Blessed be the Lord of lords and King of kings. Thank You for this sacred moment and memory of nature's praise.

May we each take a moment to bask in His presence, enjoy His creation and thank Him for His love.

Scripture Kiss:

The joy of praising God and nature praising points to the true Creator of all.

Section II: God's Intervention

Are you mindful of the magnificence of God's love and the numerous ways He expresses it to you daily?

God delights in answering our prayers. He specializes in responding to our heartfelt cries for help and He enjoys surprising us with the desires of our heart. His responses reassure us that every detail of our life is important to Him and He cares about us. He wants us to know Him personally and feel secure in His unconditional all-inclusive love.

Our Lord is aware of every detail of our life and is concerned with everything that concerns us. I pray you will become more confident in your walk with God and increase your trust and hope in Him as you read of God's interventions. By God's bestowal of mercy, grace, and blessings, you will find that God is all you need.

For the LORD God is a sun and shield; the LORD bestows favor and honor; no good thing does he withhold from those whose walk is blameless.
—Psalm 84:11 NIV.

The heavens declare the glory of God; And the firmament shows His handiwork.—Psalm 19:1

When Christ fills your life, everything will look different because you will be looking at things from His perspective. You may think life is great, but without Jesus you have no idea what you're missing out on and how great it could really be!

If you want a lasting change in your life—turn to God.

Delight yourself also in the LORD, *And He shall give you the desires of your heart.*—Psalm 37:4.

Butterfly Blanket

Some years ago a lady that I thought was my friend shared with other members of the church that I had broken her trust and had repeated things she had told me in confidence. Later it was revealed that our conversation had been overheard. It was traced to someone else divulging what they had heard her say to me. Unfortunately, a conflict over this broke out in the church family. Being a woman that considers integrity of utmost importance, I was greatly disturbed by this. People began to meddle and say some very unkind things. I went from brokenhearted to deeply distressed.

It was during this time that something interesting happened. I came across a sales magazine that had been sitting on my desk 'wish pile' for almost three years. In it was a most beautifully designed throw blanket with butterflies woven in it. It was just what I had been looking for. I really had trouble letting go of my desire for it. It was gorgeous but I considered $60.00 way too much to pay for a blanket I really didn't need. I still thought it would be a beautiful addition to our bedroom though. I admit that deep down in my heart I really wanted my

119

husband to get it for me. He didn't, but neither did he know of my desire or expectation.

I was about to throw the magazine away when I decided to take another look. It really was beautiful! I decided to call and see if by chance the price had decreased over the last three years. When I attempted to order it, I was told they had sold the last one the day before. I couldn't believe it. I said "I'll call again in a few weeks and see if someone has returned one."

About three months went by. I tried again. No blanket. I asked them for the manufactures number but they were unable to give it to me. No help. The following day I took my son to town to run an errand and while I was waiting for him I went next door to a little shop that carried Bob Timberlake throw blankets. The next day I called the manager of the shop and asked if she would try to track the butterfly throw blanket for me. She tried but to no avail. I ask her for the manufactures number and she gave it to me.

I called the manufacturer and found this was a discontinued item. They advised I try calling their retail store the next day. It was after hours for them at this time.

I wasn't able to call until about three weeks later. When I called, the young man that answered said, "Oh, I know just which one you're talking about. We had three in. The last one sold just last night. They were here when I went home last night and they're gone today." I couldn't believe it! So close two times. He promised he would check with the manager and have her check the computer for any stores that might still have one. "Don't worry. I'll keep looking for you."

He called back the following week and reported, "I'm very sorry. Nothing shows up in the computer. I'll keep my eyes open though. If one comes in, it's yours."

I told him that I'd waited three years for it and couldn't believe I was so close and had missed it. I laughingly asked him to write my phone number down in three places, so if he lost one, he would still have a copy. I confided to him that I was going to pray about it and if I was supposed to have one then it would come in and if not, I guess I wasn't supposed to have it. I thanked him and said goodbye.

I decided it was time to talk to my Father about it again. I said, "Father, You know I can live without the blanket. It is nothing I need to have. It is something that would mean very much to me. As I was speaking, I realized that if I got the blanket now it would be very much a miracle, a direct gift from God more significant now than it ever would have been before. I reflected on the picture of the blanket with that thought in mind. The spiritual connotations became increasingly significant; butterflies, new births, new beginnings. It was December. January is generally associated with new beginnings, new starts. That's what I really wanted for my marriage, for my friendships. There had been so many heartaches at church, so much rejection. I felt unaccepted, judged, misunderstood. This blanket would typify that every day can be a new day with Jesus. I don't have to keep living in the past. Each day is fresh and new. I can start over. Jesus gives new beginnings. Maybe friends don't. Maybe friends can't. Jesus does. For Jesus, if I just come to Him in willingness of spirit, accepting Him as my Savior, He covers me with His righteousness. He welcomes me just as I am, His open arms ready to help me start each new day with renewed hope and new life.

I prayed, "Father, if You want me to have this blanket, it would be very special to me now; much more than before. When I'm lonely, feeling unloved, misunderstood or unworthy, I will wrap up in my blanket and remember that no matter what, You care, and in You I am secure. Again the thought of my heartache at church came to my mind. When people talk behind your back they have trouble talking to you. It is hard for them to look you in the face. Betrayal. Pain. Distrust. Several thoughts came to my mind.

Do I have trouble looking anyone in the eyes? Do you? Is there someone who you need to confront in the spirit of Matthew 5: 23-24? It says, *Therefore if you bring your gift to the al-*

tar, and there remember that your brother has something against you, leave your gift there before the altar, and go your way. First be reconciled to your brother, and then come and offer your gift.

Are you harboring feelings of anger, resentment or bitterness toward someone who has hurt you? Do you know that no matter what anyone else thinks or feels about you, you matter to Jesus? He is eager for you to start each day fresh— forgiven and forgiving; perfectly clean, accepting and recognizing His acceptance.

While I'm writing this, I'm wrapped up in a beautiful butterfly throw blanket of God's love. The background is deep green with an array of colored flowers and butterflies around the borders and scattered within—so very gorgeous. Have you experienced the joy of being wrapped up in God's love, tangibly as well as in your heart? Is there something small that you have, or that you could get, that can be a visual reminder for you when you are low, that God loves you? He loves you. He loves you. No matter what, He loves you.

God sent me the blanket on sale for $19.99!!! When this young man called to tell me he had found it, I just squealed! I told him thank you over and over again. I said, "You've gone out of your way for me so much on this, I just can't believe it. Are you a Christian?"

He stammered, "Well, sort of. I don't go to church really. I was raised Catholic."

I retorted, "Well, would you please get your act together? Get right with God, because He's coming soon and I want to meet you! You've been wonderful.

He responded, "Are you in California?"

"Yes."

"Well I'm moving out to San Francisco in about three months. (He was in North Carolina.) How far are you from there?"

"About three hours." I said.

"Maybe we will be able to meet." he replied excitedly.

I asked, "Where's your family? (I think he said they were in Oklahoma.) Well then, take my phone number and put it in your pocket. We're the parents of seven boys and we have taken in a lot of children. If you don't have any family out here you might need a surrogate family. Call us when you move."

He said, "Okay." (Unfortunately we never met.) Now I have a butterfly blanket I had wanted for three years as a gift from God, for a third of the price. It carries with it comfort, warmth, love, and reassurance because of the spiritual significance now attached to it. Let's curl up and talk about my best friend Jesus. Have you met Him? I think He's wonderful. Guess what? There's no question about it. He loves us!

Every good gift and every perfect gift is from above, coming down from the Father of lights, with whom can be no variation, neither shadow that is cast by turning.—James 1:17 ASV.

Intervention Kiss:

God delights in giving us the desires of our hearts. Every piece of this journey in obtaining the blanket—from finding it in the magazine to pursuing it, then taking possession of it were all exciting moments with God.

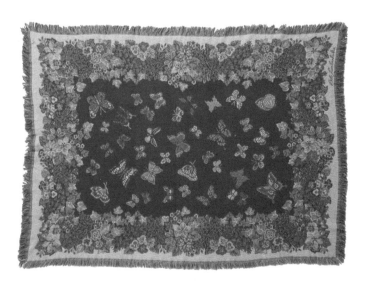

With Kisses From Heaven

The sweetest kiss was Jesus making me wait so He could attach spiritual significance to His gift and engulf me in His arms of love as I am wrapped in the blanket.

Then Samuel took a flask of oil and poured it *on his head, and kissed him and said: "Is* it *not because the LORD has anointed you ...?*
—1 Samuel 10:1.

"I know your works. See, I have set before you an open door, and no one can shut it; for you have a little strength, have kept My word, and have not denied My name.—Revelation 3:8.

The most dramatic changes in your life will come from God's initiative, not yours.
—Henry Blackaby, *Experiencing God,* p211

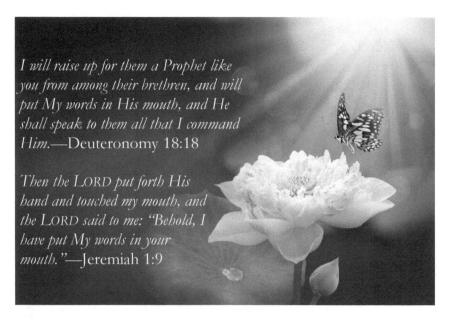

I will raise up for them a Prophet like you from among their brethren, and will put My words in His mouth, and He shall speak to them all that I command Him.—Deuteronomy 18:18

Then the LORD put forth His hand and touched my mouth, and the LORD said to me: "Behold, I have put My words in your mouth."—Jeremiah 1:9

Called To Speak

When the Lord asked me to start speaking and prepare business cards and brochures, I ran from Him for three months. He was persistent. I was certain His assignment was way over my head. Finally I sat down to have a chat with God. I told Him quite emphatically, "Father, Please no. It's too big a job for a little girl. I can't do this. Besides I'm scared. I don't know what you want me to do. My schedule is really full, Lord."

God first tugged at my heart in October, then in November and then in December. Again I defended myself with, "Father, do you know what time of the year it is? You're asking me to get business cards and brochures ready. I can't do this, not now. I need a logo and motto. The holidays are here and I am overloaded with extra things to do and activities the boys are participating in. I'm too divided to concentrate on something this important.

In January, when His voice became only a whisper, I got nervous. With concern, I timidly insisted, "Father, please don't withdraw Your Spirit. I promise I'll do it this month."

The end of the month came and I was suddenly jarred. I hadn't done any work on the logo or motto. I sat on the side of my bed and prayed. "Father, I promised You I would have this done for You by today. Here I am. I don't know where to begin. I can't do this without You. Please help me."

I no sooner got the words out of my mouth when I heard "Freedom In Surrender."

"Freedom In Surrender!" I love it Lord. It's me. It's what I long for and try to do for You—surrender.

Now Jesus, I need a logo."

During that time, I had gone to my room and another parent was teaching our homeschooled children. It was 'Opportunity Plus Day.' This meant that community homeschoolers and their parents gathered at our home and took turns teaching their specialty. Today a class on sign language was being presented.

I joined the class. As I pulled up my chair, God gave me a quick picture of the logo. So quick, I asked for a replay. Now I needed to have someone help me draw it.

I thanked Jesus for His guidance and promised to go the next day to a design artist and get things started. It was a great meeting and I was excited. We made a follow-up appointment and she got busy on the project.

Before our next appointment, I had weekend company scheduled. My mother, coming from Oregon was bringing relatives with her that I had never met. One evening as we were sharing, I told Mom what was going on with preparations for the brochures and business cards that God had told me to make. I shared what the logo was and that it was in the design stage … but I wasn't happy with how the script for the words "Freedom In Surrender" looked. I asked Mom to give it a try. She had lovely penmanship.

Part of it looked right. Part of it didn't. One of our guests came by and said, "May I try?"

126

God brought total strangers to my home to help me with the script for the logo. Part of 'Freedom in Surrender' ended up in my Mom's handwriting and part of it is his. I knew the minute I saw it. This is it!!!

When I took it in at the next appointment with my designer, she loved it. She showed me what she had done with the cross and dove. The dove wasn't right. I prayed, "Please show me. Please help me know when it is what You want."

While she was doodling she said, "Derry, I don't have anything else to give you. I don't know where to go from here. Maybe, you need to try someone else."

As she finished speaking I put my head down in disappointment. I really liked her. I glanced over at her doodles and in excitement exclaimed, "That's it. That's it! You have it. Now I just need you to put them together." There amidst all her doodles was the perfect dove.

God gave her the inspired doodle that became part of the logo.

Unfortunately, until we become more mature in our walk with God, it takes some of us a little longer to obey immediately. It takes us a little longer to do what God wants us to do; to listen to His voice. When we do, we become new people in Him. Relationship with Him transforms us. He has a plan and destiny for each of us that no one else can fill. His plan is a plan to bring us fullness of joy and will give us a sense of accomplishment as we trust in Him. God called me to speak and He was preparing the way.

And I have put My words in your mouth; I have covered you with the shadow of My hand, That I may plant the heavens, Lay the foundations of the earth, And say to Zion, 'You are My people.— Isaiah 51:16.

For I have not spoken on My own authority; but the Father who sent Me gave Me a command, what I should say and what I should speak
—John 12:49.

127

With Kisses From Heaven

Intervention Kiss:

When God calls, He enables. He doesn't want us to fail. He wants us to succeed. He puts everything together if we listen and wait upon Him.

 Butterfly Kiss:

Life Lessons From A Butterfly

Let go of the past ...
Trust the future ...
Embrace change ...
Come out of the cocoon ...
Unfurl your wings ...
Dare to get off the ground ...
Ride the breeze ...
Savor the flowers ...
Put on your brightest colors ...
Let your beauty show.
—Meghan Makenzie

The thief's purpose is to steal and kill and destroy. My purpose is to give them a rich and satisfying life.
    —John 10:10 NLT

Choking On A Banana

My first born was an absolute delight. I always wanted to be a mother and now I held my first treasure in my arms. Anyone who would meet him now would never guess that he entered the world a month early weighing in at 5 lbs 4 oz, dropping to 4 lbs 6 oz. He is one big guy now!

Starting life outside of his protective chamber earlier than the expected nine months brought with it some digestive problems. He suffered severely with colic. His tummy tightened and brought him much pain.

He was a prayed-for baby and as my firstborn I knew God had a special plan for his life. Praying parents can pray a hedge of protection over their children. I had for him. I also prayed perseveringly for his digestive system.

When the doctor directed me to start giving him cereal and mashed bananas, I hoped he would be able to handle it. He seemed to enjoy the banana. Often I would put a little banana on his highchair tray and mash it as I fed it to him.

One day, he must have grabbed a piece when I looked away, because when I put the next bite in he wouldn't take it. Then I saw that he didn't seem to be breathing. I started patting his back. Nothing. I quickly grabbed him out of his highchair and patted his back harder. He was turning blue now and I was beginning to panic. I checked his mouth and couldn't see anything. I did a sweep of his little mouth with my finger and tried to check his throat. I turned him upside down and pounded on his back. Nothing. He is getting bluer. I am crying out to God yelling for help. Finally—out popped a piece of banana! I sat down and held him close. We were both crying. Sobbing, I thanked God for saving my son's life.

My precious baby had been choking on a banana. People can die from choking. I could have lost him, but thanks be to God, his life was spared.

God saved his life. God can save your life as well. He can save your life for eternity if you will call upon Him.

Intervention Kisses:

I thank God for the gift of my son and for protecting his life. Thank You Father for the joy he brings into my life and the love and caring he extends my way. May he serve You with all his heart and continue to lead His sons into a saving relationship with You

The LORD *is good to all, and his compassion is over all that he has made.*
   —Psalm 145:9 RSV

Compassion Brings Disappointment

Being the oldest child in the family had some real advantages. In my particular case, as the firstborn I was Daddy's favorite and being a girl I got a lot of his attention. Another benefit of being Daddy's favorite and the oldest child was that he wanted to take me on special events with him—like his hunting trips. He used to take me to hunt ducks in the meadow. I was to retrieve whatever he shot.

I would do it for my dad, but it was scary. Sometimes, when the other hunters hadn't heard my dad call out that I would be retrieving; I would hear bullets that had missed their mark dropping near me.

Dad liked to go deer hunting, too. He was eagerly looking forward to me accompanying him. In order to go hunting for venison—deer meat—I had to be properly prepared. Dad decided to enroll me in a rifle safety class. If I passed, I was promised my own .22 gauge rifle, a .22 pistol and a .30-30. That was a lot of incentive to excel.

I was under a lot of pressure. I was the only girl and the youngest in class. I was 12 and all the guys were in their teens.

They all seemed amused that I was in the class. In their eyes I offered no threat.

How surprised we all were at the end of the class when the teacher called me up and congratulated me as the only student that had received a perfect score! I received the only 'A' given. My dad was so proud, he planned a hunting trip for us the following week.

I have vivid and distinct memories of that trip!!! Dad woke me up at four in the morning. It was cold and dark outside. We left bundled up and drove several hours. When we arrived at our destination it was barely sunrise. The smell of sagebrush in the damp morning dew was strong.

We started out slowly, climbing one hill after another. It turned into a long arduous hike. With my short legs, those hills felt like mountains. The day went from cool to uncomfortably hot.

Except for the birds and an occasional rabbit, nature was quiet. There was no evidence of deer tracks, either. We stopped for lunch and rested in the shade. As we talked and planned the rest of our day, Dad seemed determined that we wouldn't return home until we had "my" deer. I was ready to call it quits.

At the end of a long day and no luck in our hunting expedition we are about to stop when Dad said, "One more hill. We're just going to go over one more hill."

As we crested the top of the next hill we stopped and surveyed the area. There were more hills, but on the hill directly across from us stood a beautiful four- forked buck. He was just standing there on the top of the hill looking at us.

My heart started pounding. I was excited. Dad had told me that if we saw one, it was mine. My dad instructed me, "All right, sweetheart, this one is for you. Take your time. Raise your gun slowly. Point your gun in his direction. Get him in your sights. Slowly squeeze the trigger."

Compassion Brings Disappointment

I raised my gun, pointed it in the right direction, looked through the sights, but ... I couldn't pull the trigger. I saw the deer was centered right in the crosshairs of my sight but all I could do is just stare at him there. My dad said, "Take your time, honey. He's just standing there waiting for you. Line him up. When you're ready, squeeze that trigger. Now, Derry. Pull the trigger. Pull it *NOW*." But I couldn't.

Suddenly the whole story of the movie Bambi flashed through my mind. It seemed impossible to shoot the star.

I was 12 years old. I wasn't used to attending church but Mom read us Bible stories before bed and we rehearsed the prayer "Now I lay me down to sleep."

Staring at the deer on the top of the hill, I cried out to Jesus. "Please save him. Please help him run away." Just as my father raised his rifle, my 'Bambi' ran away.

Today, as a woman who knows Jesus, the verses in Psalm 36:6-7 RSV seem fitting here. *Thy righteousness is like the mountains of God, thy judgments are like the great deep; man and beast thou savest, O LORD. How precious is thy steadfast love, O God! ...* My Father in heaven heard the cry of my heart and answered a little girl's prayer.

My father was not happy with me. Although he understood my sensitive and compassionate heart, he was still very disappointed. When we got home he took my rifle and the handguns he had given me. I never saw them again and I never asked for them.

Intervention Kiss:

God heard the cry of a little girl's heart and protected a beautiful buck from meeting its demise that day. God will hear the cry of your heart as well.

John answered and said, "A man can receive nothing unless it has been given to him from heaven.—John 3:27.

Yesterday's confidence is not enough for today's challenges. The Lord gives the day and shows the way.

    —Lloyd Ogilvie, *God's Best For My Life,*
      July 25

They speak falsehood to one another;
With flattering lips and with a double
heart they speak.
　　　—Psalm 12:2 NASB

Crooked Deal

I had a call one day from a gal that I had previously worked with. She was having some financial difficulties and wondered if her daughter could come live with us for a while. She knew I was doing homeschooling. Her daughter had fallen behind in her schoolwork and she thought I might be able to help her catch up to her classmates. There were a few other issues her daughter was dealing with which she hoped I would be able to address and guide her through.

After she left my home I helped her daughter settle in. As we started putting her clothes away, I was surprised at how little she had. The next day we went clothes shopping. After raising seven sons, I found it an entirely different experience taking a young eight-year-old girl shopping for clothes.

Heidi was quickly acclimated, applied herself and did well. The time flew by quickly. Before we realized it, her mom was there to pick her up and take her home to her new place. As her mom and I were visiting she mentioned that her new boyfriend was a used car salesman. That sparked my interest. We had two old cars—relics that had been parked in the yard for some time and a cab-over camper and pickup that we had been talking about getting rid of. She said she was sure her boyfriend could help us sell them.

I ran the idea of the car sales by my husband and we were in agreement that this was a great opportunity. Heidi's mom, Katie and her boyfriend Rob made arrangements to pick up the vehicles over a period of two weeks. Because I had known Katie for many years, and because she had trusted me with her daughter I knew I could trust her. In order to make the sale of the vehicles uncomplicated, I turned over the registration papers and pink slips.

Weeks went by and there was no word. When I finally caught up with her, there was not a good report. Nothing had sold yet. Months later I had difficulty getting in touch with her. More months went by. Her phone number had been disconnected.

My husband and I were headed out of town on a trip. We had to drive two and a half hours to San Francisco to catch the plane. On the way there we started talking about the cars that had been taken and were supposedly on a lot in San Francisco somewhere. We both got the same brainstorm at the same time. We would delay our trip for a day and see if we could track down our friends and our cars.

We stopped and prayed about our change of plans and this new excursion. We claimed the promise in Jeremiah 33:3, *'Call to Me, and I will answer you, and show you great and mighty things, which you do not know.'*

Our investigative adventure began. We prayed each step of the way. We started out visiting the last address I had for her. They had moved but we got a lead and followed it; got another lead and followed it. One after another, one place after another. We finally found where Rob had worked and got a lead to where he was transferred. This detective work together was exciting!!!

136

Rob was so shocked when he saw us show up at the car dealership that he turned pale. He was speechless. Fortunately for us he was with a client, so I asked him for Kate's address. He wrote it down and said he would be there shortly. We headed to her apartment. Her greeting was, "How dare you track me down like a common criminal."

Hmmm, that was certainly a clue that there was more to this story than we yet knew. We had become the victims of a crooked deal!

It ended up that the truck and camper had sold and the two antique cars were hidden. The papers had been forged! The location of the cars was revealed. We got the legal papers back, made arrangements for the cars to get picked up and sold them within a few weeks.

What a bitter disappointment that someone I had both trusted and helped, with an open and devoted heart, would deceive me and rob me. I could have turned her in for forgery. Knowing that if she had to serve time Heidi would be placed in foster care, I chose not to file charges against her. I have prayed that she would have a repentant and transformed heart and once again be a woman of integrity, thankful that she was spared the consequences of her actions and wrong decisions.

Intervention Kisses:

God, the Revealer of Secrets, led and directed us step by step to recover our stolen property. While we were 'investigating' and having fun playing detectives our marriage strengthened, our friendship grew and we were more unified.

While I am thankful that the cars sold quickly once back in our possession, the biggest kiss from the Lord was He enabled us to forgive immediately. If there is something you need God to reveal to you—ask Him!

The people God used mightily in Scripture were all ordinary people to whom He gave divine assignments they never could have initiated.

—Henry Blackaby, *Experiencing God,* p211

 Butterfly Kiss:

HAPPINESS.—A butterfly, which when pursued, seems always just beyond your grasp; but if you sit down quietly, may alight upon you.

—"L," *The Daily Crescent*

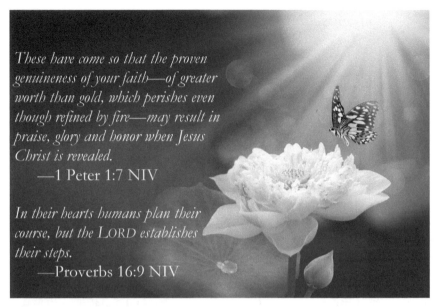

These have come so that the proven genuineness of your faith—of greater worth than gold, which perishes even though refined by fire—may result in praise, glory and honor when Jesus Christ is revealed.
    —1 Peter 1:7 NIV

In their hearts humans plan their course, but the LORD establishes their steps.
    —Proverbs 16:9 NIV

Eleventh Hour

When I gave my heart to Jesus as an adult, after learning that He is a personal God that loves me and cares about everything that concerns me, I was experiencing so many incredible answers to prayer and had such an exciting testimony, I was asked to share it in church services around our community and surrounding areas. I thoroughly enjoyed sharing my new found love of Jesus with others. It thrilled my heart to be able to offer them hope and encouragement.

One evening, I had just given my testimony for the eleventh time in a church meeting setting when the enemy, the devil, wiggled into my thoughts and caused me to temporarily stumble.

I was standing at the outside doors shaking hands with people as they departed, listening to their positive remarks about the encouragement they had received from the stories I had shared of God's interventions in my life. A lady took my hand, held it between her two hands and looked me in the eyes, "You must be pretty special for God to work like this in your life dear."

Without warning, the thought came to me, "I must be pretty special. Why don't any of these people have a story to tell?"

I had a 35-minute drive home. For the first ten or fifteen minutes I was really chewing on this new thought, 'I must be pretty special.' It didn't take me long to make myself sick … of me. By the time I got home I fell across my bed in tears asking God to forgive me for my inflated opinion of myself. I told Him I would never speak again because I could not be trusted. I said, "I waited too long to find You. I will not let myself become prideful and loose out on eternity. This is as though it is the eleventh hour for me. I will not lose You. I will let You purify my heart."

My heart was broken because I couldn't be trusted to speak for Him. I stepped back. Fifteen years later a local Christian college asked if I would speak for their chapel meeting. Most of the young people there were like a part of our family. They referred to me as Mom James. They spent many weekends at our home. We studied the Bible together, worked and played. We got to know each other pretty well. When the college dean called and asked me to speak to them before they headed home on break, I readily agreed.

It wasn't until the day I was scheduled to share at Chapel that it hit me between the eyes—I was speaking again. It hadn't felt that way because they were family to us. It was like having family worship together.

In two days the students would be leaving for their two-week Christmas break. The deans had been concerned about them because some were going back to some serious family problems. I went ahead and shared what God had given me for them and prayed a blessing covering them during their vacation.

That day at the college I was invited to come back the following month. I asked them to let me check my calendar and I would get back to them.

On the way home I reminded God that I wasn't going to speak for Him again and I couldn't be trusted. He reminded me that I belonged to Him and He had had me in training. I was now ready. I thought of the text in 2 Corinthians 5:17 NIV, *Therefore, if anyone is in Christ, that person is a new creation: The old has gone, the new is here!* and thanked God that I was a new creation in Him.

It was shortly after that when He began urging me to prepare my business cards and brochures. That's another story. You can read about it in this book. The story is "Called to Speak."

God in His grace, mercy and love works in us to sanctify us for His service. We have each been called to a special and individual work for His Kingdom. We are each special to Him. We are all in training, and if we are willing, He will use us as we grow and learn. He isn't waiting for perfection. He is waiting for a willing and yielded heart.

May God himself, the God of peace, sanctify you through and through. May your whole spirit, soul and body be kept blameless at the coming of our Lord Jesus Christ.—1 Thessalonians 5:23 NIV.

Intervention Kisses:

God once again intervened in my life reminding me that He has a destiny and purpose for me as He does for each person.

My failures didn't stop God from reaching out to me and calling me to service again for His Kingdom. His unconditional love looks into our heart and reaches out in compassion at our human failings, standing us back up on our feet and giving us marching orders.

We are all special to Jesus. Will we let God be Lord of our lives, or will we hide in shame from our mistakes and disappointments?

God is continually doing and giving for us, for our best interest, for our delight, for our care and pleasure—to offer encouragement, protection or provision to make life easier.

Oh give thanks to the LORD, call upon His name; Make known His deeds among the peoples.—1 Chronicles 16:8 NASB.

The angel of the LORD encamps all around those who fear Him, And delivers them.—Psalm 34:7

'Call to Me, and I will answer you, and show you great and mighty things, which you do not know.'—Jeremiah 33:3

Fireworks Under The House

I had been having some electrical problems in the dining room. The lights kept flickering. I finally succumbed to calling an electrician friend.

He spent some time checking through things in the house and couldn't find anything. Then I remembered something I hoped would be of help. There was a light that my husband had previously mounted in the crawl space under the dining room. I wondered if that might be contributing to our problem in any way.

I can't remember whether it did. What I do remember is that God used the flickering lights to reveal two much larger unknown and serious problems.

When the electrician went under the house he came upon an open electrical wire that was intermittently sparking. Thank God he saw the spark before he happened to crawl over it. He could have been electrocuted!!!

It had been sparking for some time and the burn marks showed on the beams. While he was under the house he happened to notice that because of the way the fireplace had been left during construction, hot ashes were dropping down under the house as well and a portion of the floor joist had been burned through.

By the grace of God, he came across these areas of previous "fireworks" under the house. How thankful I am that I serve a God who protects us and is a revealer of secrets. This could have gone on until we had a real fire going. What if it had happened while I was away at work, or while we were sleeping?

Jesus promises to send His angels to watch over us...and they sure did. Two dangerous situations were revealed and corrected. God had protected our lives and property!

Intervention Kiss:

Thank you, precious Lord for protecting our lives and our home. Won't it be fun to go to heaven, sit and visit with Jesus and find out how and when our lives were protected unbeknown to us? Thank Him now for what you don't know!

 ## Butterfly Kiss:

There is nothing in a caterpillar that tells you it's going to be a butterfly.

—R. Buckminster Fuller

And Peter said to them, "Repent, and be baptized every one of you in the name of Jesus Christ for the forgiveness of your sins; and you shall receive the gift of the Holy Spirit.
—Acts 2:38 RSV

Glory

The agenda for the week was already full. But some things, unexpected as they were, took precedence. When Thomas called requesting baptism, I answered, "Wonderful! When would you like to do this?"

His response surprised me, "Today."

"Today?"

"Yes. I am being deployed this weekend and I want to be baptized before I leave."

"Well, let me talk to Pastor Ron and see what time he is available. Are your parents going to be able to come? And when could you do it? It usually takes half a day to fill the baptistery, unless you want to go to a lake somewhere."

"I can do it anytime. My folks are out of town. I just want to do this alone, but I would like you and Pastor Ron to do it together. A lake would be great."

"Okay. Let me check with him and get back to you."

Shortly after the call, we worked out the time and place. The lake was about 25 minutes away. It was a gray day with a lot of clouds in the sky. I wondered how cold the water would be.

We arrived in our baptismal gowns, Bibles in hand. When we got out of the car, people in the next car said, "Oh, a baptism. Can we come watch?"

I said to Thomas, "Well, you wanted it quiet, but God wants you to testify. He already has some first fruits for you Thomas."

We dropped the towels along the shore and waded out. Cold, oh so cold. But I looked up in the sky and whispered quietly to God, "Oh Lord, it would be so wonderful if when we raise Thomas out of the water, the sun would break through and beams of light would shine down on him."

And that is exactly what happened. God answered my prayer and smiled His light down on Thomas. It was as though he was shrouded in glory.

When we came back to the car, a middle aged man was sitting in his car next to us crying. He said, "It's been so long since I've walked with God. Today shows me that I need to make some serious changes in my life. I've become an alcoholic. My marriage is all but destroyed. My wife doesn't want me anymore. I haven't been a descent dad to my children. I came here to be alone, but God called to me by witnessing this baptism."

In Matthew 10:32 Jesus says, *"Therefore whoever confesses Me before men, him I will also confess before My Father who is in heaven.* That day Thomas, who had no intention of having his baptism witnessed by others, made deposits in two people's hearts for the kingdom of God. And, in answer to this scripture promise, the Lord set him up for more blessings ahead.

Have you committed your life to Jesus? Have you made a public proclamation through baptism that your life is now surrendered to Him? If you do, you too will receive a kiss from heaven…maybe not the same way as Thomas, but things will be different.

146

A man's heart plans his way, But the LORD directs his steps.
—Proverbs 16:9

Intervention Kisses:

What a glorious moment for Thomas. Heaven was shining on him through God's demonstration of His presence and His joy over Thomas's decision. The hearts of those on shore observing the baptism were moved to make life-changing decisions. Heaven rejoices over each of us when we choose to make Him Lord of our lives.

Thank you for touching so many lives, Father.

 Butterfly Kiss:

Butterflies are nature's angels, they remind us what a gift it is to be alive.
—Robyn Nola.

Yes, the LORD will give what is *good;* ...—Psalm 85:12.

Don't let the busyness of your present activity keep you from experiencing all that God has in store for you.

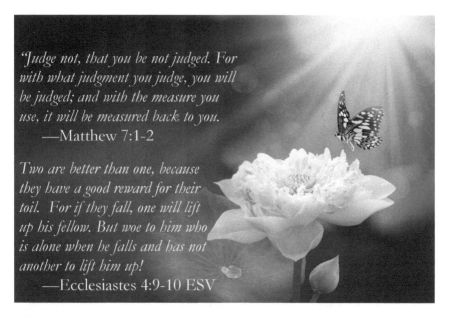

"Judge not, that you be not judged. For with what judgment you judge, you will be judged; and with the measure you use, it will be measured back to you.
—Matthew 7:1-2

Two are better than one, because they have a good reward for their toil. For if they fall, one will lift up his fellow. But woe to him who is alone when he falls and has not another to lift him up!
—Ecclesiastes 4:9-10 ESV

God Sent A Mouse

My heart was torn. I felt very alone. Even though I had been previously excited and knew God had answered my prayers and had opened the doors of opportunity for me to go to college, I was now apprehensive.

I had gotten a ride to college with a relative. On the way there we had stopped by the market so I could stock up on a few snacks. I was then dropped off with all my baggage. I knew no one there and my surroundings were unfamiliar.

I soon found that summer students were placed in the basement apartments because there was no air conditioning in the dorm and they were cooler. I had accepted three jobs and started work that afternoon so had no time to get my room in order. Each room came equipped with two beds, two dressers and two desks. When I arrived the furniture was piled in the middle of the room. I unloaded my groceries on the closet shelf and headed to my first job at the cafeteria.

While I wanted to make friends, I held back, I think partly because of the emotional turmoil churning in my heart.

I was sad that my mother hadn't been able to bring me, see where I would be living and share setting up my room with me. Unfortunately, feeling a bit insecure, I became self-protective and began scrutinizing those around me, forming opinions and judgments. Not a good start to building healthy relationships!

There was one girl there who immediately caught my attention and triggered a negative reaction in me. Carol was a stocky blonde girl—taller than I—with a bubble haircut. She seemed to walk around in a trance—her own world. She didn't seem to be cognizant of anyone around her. She shuffled at a slow pace humming a little tune to herself; la la la la la la la! She took her time doing her job and didn't seem very knowledgeable doing kitchen responsibilities. I unfairly summed her up as a "space cadet" and dismissed her.

I had been assigned a number of things to accomplish for the next meal and I needed to get to it. I would have plenty of time to reach out to others I worked with once I got my footing. Interesting that while I was making determinations based upon first opinions, it didn't occur to me that "first impressions" were just as important when others looked in my direction.

At the end of my shift, I was worn out. It had been a long drive there, was very hot outside with no air conditioning in the dorm rooms, and I had yet to get furniture placed and my bed made up. I couldn't wait to take a shower and lay down with a book. I started my other two jobs the next day.

Once back to my room I decided to break into my stash of cinnamon rolls before I jumped into interior decorating! I reached up to the shelf in my closet for a roll and jumped back startled and screaming. A *mouse* leaped down from the shelf right in front of me and began spinning around in circles in the middle of my room.

I had not yet become a country girl! In fact, I was very much a city girl at that time. I knew nothing about mice except what I had seen in cartoons. I only knew that when a mouse is present, you climb on the highest object available. I headed for my dresser—still in the middle of the room—climbed on top of it and surveyed the area for the mouse, wondering what to do next. I just stood there—in fear, expecting the mouse to attempt climbing up my leg! What was I going to do? The dorm was quiet. There didn't seem to be anyone down here in the basement area. It all seemed a bit spooky and I felt very undone and vulnerable.

Fortunately my door was open, wide open. I watched the doorway hoping the mouse would run out. No such luck. Where did he go? Even from my vantage point I couldn't detect his whereabouts. I was beginning to feel foolish and was contemplating how to resolve this problem when suddenly help arrived. Help that was humiliating to me!!!

As I stood there searching for alternatives, the tall blonde came strolling by—eyes straight ahead, la la la la la la la! I didn't move. I didn't speak. Then just as she had passed by, she backed up. Not turned around—backed up! With one foot behind the other as if in reverse, eyes still forward—she backed up! Then turned her head and just looked at me. "What are you doing up there?" Carol questioned.

"A mouse." I responded with a frown.

"A mouse?" she smirked in wonder.

"A mouse. There's a mouse in my room." I retorted.

"Where is it?" she asked

"I don't know. I can't find it." I replied, embarrassed.

"Do you have a broom?" she asked.

"In my closet," I responded.

Carol went to my closet and got the broom. She held it over her shoulder and began chanting, "Here little mousey, mousey. Here little mousey, mousey." Then she looked up at me laughing and said, "I'll cover for you. You come on down." So I did!

With Kisses From Heaven

It seemed to me I had no other option but to follow her instructions. I was next ordered to get myself a change of clothes and grab my sheets, towels and toiletries and told I could spend the night in her room. Unbelievable!!! I was going to spend the night sharing a room with Carol—of all people!

That night was the beginning of a lifelong friendship. God is sometimes hysterical!!! I have asked Him to choose my friends for me and so He does, even if it means using a mouse to bring people together. Thank You God for intervening!!! Amazing love!

Carol and I became college roommates and after our first year of college we got an apartment together and worked at the hospital to earn money for our next year of education. We learned survival tactics together and helped each other grow and mature. We were accountability friends and became each other's confidant. Proverbs 27:9 NIV says, *Perfume and incense bring joy to the heart, and the pleasantness of a friend springs from their heartfelt advice.* We proved that to be true. We also experienced Proverbs 27:17 NIV to be true, *As iron sharpens iron, so one person sharpens another.*

In living and sharing together we learned the importance of the advice in Colossians 3:12-14 RSV, *Put on then, as God's chosen ones, holy and beloved, compassion, kindness, lowliness, meekness, and patience, forbearing one another and, if one has a complaint against another, forgiving each other; as the Lord has forgiven you, so you also must forgive. And above all these put on love, which binds everything together in perfect harmony.*

Now, some 55 years later Carol and I are still supporting and encouraging each other through life's journey. Job 16:20-21 NIV is being fulfilled in our friendship even though separated by thousands of miles *My intercessor is my friend as my eyes pour out tears to God; on behalf of a man he pleads with God as one pleads for a friend.*

But even this is not the end. Soon and very soon our Lord is returning to take us home with Him and I will have the privilege of spending eternity with this precious godly woman that God gave me as a gift so very long ago.

That makes me think of the little poem by Joseph Parry (1841-1903). "Make new friends, but keep the old. One is silver and the other gold." Because of my own insecurities and frame of mind way back then, I  almost missed out on a wonderful golden friendship. My judgments of Carol were so wrong!!! Perhaps that is why God instructs us not to judge one another. I thank God that He knows me. He understands my heart and is aware of what and whom I need in my life.

His wisdom, vision and perspective helps us to evaluate our contribution to relationships. Do we cherish our friends or take them for granted? Do we show them mercy and grace or judge them? Do we forgive quickly or carry grudges and make them grovel? Do we give them space to be who God created them to be and encourage them in it or do we begrudge their gifts and talents and respond with jealousy? Do we open our arms to new friendships formed by them or are we possessive and threatened? Do we follow Jesus example of friendship and love unconditionally securing "forever" friendships?

Intervention Kisses:

The Bible is clear in 1 Corinthians 15:33 NIV. *Do not be misled: "Bad company corrupts good character."* Only our loving God, Who has our best interest in mind, will lead us to healthy, positive people for lasting friendships. Thank You, Jesus.

May you seek and enjoy God's wisdom as you form relationships.

He who did not spare His own Son, but delivered Him up for us all, how shall He not with Him also freely give us all things?—Romans 8:32.

He who gives a right answer kisses the lips.—Proverbs 24:26.

There is no limit of power available to a person who is willing to give God the glory and leave the results to Him.

—Lloyd Ogilvie, *God's Best For My Life,*
July 28

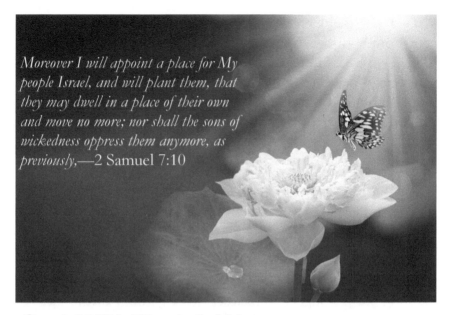

Moreover I will appoint a place for My people Israel, and will plant them, that they may dwell in a place of their own and move no more; nor shall the sons of wickedness oppress them anymore, as previously,—2 Samuel 7:10

God Will Find A Way

After 22 years I couldn't believe I had listened to my husband's confession again, had witnessed his impatience with my inability to accept his secondary lifestyle, and now the silence of the house; silence interrupted by my cries of anguish.

I had been suspicious for a while, but had been walking in denial. I had finally come to the place where I was brave enough to ask God to reveal secrets to me, as He promises in Jeremiah 33:3, *'Call to Me, and I will answer you, and show you great and mighty things which you do not know.'*

Now that He had, I was in turmoil and heartache. I couldn't believe that my husband would choose Mother's Day to break the news. How dare he. We had been gone most of the day and our son had been home working on a special meal for me. He had spent hours in the kitchen making a very creative and delicious meal, setting a beautiful table for two in a romantic atmosphere for us. How dare my husband break this news to me on the way up the driveway and expect me to be able to hold it together. I was filled with anger and pain.

With Kisses From Heaven

I was thanking God for answering my prayer, but now I cried out with new appeals. "If ever I needed you Lord, it is now," I sobbed. "I need Your strength, Your protection, Your provision. I need Your help to love with Your love and forgive with Your forgiveness. Please give me abundant wisdom, but at this moment I most need Your comfort. Like David in Psalm 138:8 and Psalm 73:26, I cry out, Lord, You have promised to *perfect what concerns me* and not forsake me. Though my heart fails me, You are *the strength of my heart and my portion forever.*

Living through the intense pain, turbulence, and instability of this marriage and then being alone, rejected and betrayed, was difficult even with God holding me and guiding me. It is hard to imagine the depth of suffering a person can endure going through this on their own without divine intervention.

God helped me over and over, in my despair, in my fears, in my humiliation. I clung to the Bible promise He showed me in Isaiah 54:5-10, *For your Maker is your Husband, the LORD of Hosts is His name; And your Redeemer is the Holy One of Israel; He is called the God of the whole earth. For the LORD has called you Like a woman forsaken and grieved in spirit, Like a youthful wife when you were refused," Says your God. "For a mere moment I have forsaken you, But with great mercies I will gather you. With a little wrath I hid My face from you for a moment; But with everlasting kindness I will have mercy on you," Says the LORD, your Redeemer. "For this is like the waters of Noah to Me; For as I have sworn That the waters of Noah would no longer cover the earth, So have I sworn That I would not be angry with you, nor rebuke you. For the mountains shall depart And the hills be removed, But My kindness shall not depart from you, Nor shall My covenant of peace be removed," Says the LORD, who has mercy on you.* As I daily claimed this promise I was assured that God was by my side and I would get through this.

Working through the divorce agreements was exhausting and heart wrenching. When we got down to the house and what should be done, I once again deferred to God's guidance.

156

We were in settlement discussions with our attorneys. My attorney and I had been fasting and praying. It was time for the opposition to return from lunch. I went into the Ladies Room and cried out to God. You haven't told me what to do. I am out of time. I need to know now whether you want me to keep the house. Clearly God said, "Keep it." Then I began to cry. "Lord, I can't. This is too much for a little girl. I can't do this." God said, "Trust Me." All this happened on a Wednesday.

My flesh and my heart fail; But *God* is *the strength of my heart and my portion forever.*—Psalm 73:26

On the following Sunday, within 30 minutes of each other, I had two young adults knock at my door and ask if they could rent a room from me. They did not know each other. I sat there in awe. I had no idea what to charge them. I tossed out a monthly amount. They both shook their heads. They were not willing to pay that. They said they had been looking and the going price for less space and accommodations than I offered them was going for substantially more. Therefore, they offered more than I asked and moved in that week.

Once again God was providing for my needs. He directed me to keep the house which meant I had to take out a mortgage to buy it from my husband. Now God was placing two very special young people in His home to help me pay the monthly mortgage payment. God found a way—and surprised me with His goodness and provision. In Philippians 4:13 we are promised *I can do all things through Christ who strengthens me.* Through His love and divine intervention that is true, if we will just trust in Him.

With Kisses From Heaven

Intervention Kisses:

God intervened on my behalf and gave me the courage to trust Him as He guided me through my heartaches and challenges, then provided a way. This was just the beginning of God's continual help and provision. He never failed me. What He did for me, He will do for you. Trust and obey.

 Butterfly Kiss:

What the caterpillar calls the end of the world, the master calls a butterfly.

—Richard Bach

For every beast of the forest is Mine,
And the cattle on a thousand hills. I
know all the birds of the mountains,
And the wild beasts of the field are
Mine.—Psalm 50:10-11

Kisses From Nature

Some "kisses from heaven" are brief but precious. Many brief "kisses" are encounters with nature. Under this title I will share a number of those interesting and precious moments of nature "kisses" in my life.

Nature encounter "kiss" number one:

Jesus said to them, "Children, have you any fish?" They answered him, "No." He said to them, "Cast the net on the right side of the boat, and you will find some." ...—John 21:5-6 RSV.

There is something special about "firsts." Your first birthday. The first tooth that comes out. Your first day at school. The first time Dad and Mom allowed you to do something you have looked forward to. Your first date, your first kiss, your first child, etc. etc.

One first that stands out in my mind is the day I caught my first fish. My dad was a hunter and fisherman. I was his right-hand girl. The family was backpacking in for a special weekend up in the mountains. Dad knew a place by the side of the river that he thought would be a good place for our family to stay. It was a great river with a shoreline that enabled us— the children—to wade in and play in the water safely while my folks could go a bit upstream within sight, and fish.

We arrived near the spot Dad had in mind. He instructed us to wait where we were and he would hike a bit farther to check out the area.

During the day we had stopped occasionally for a "fishing" break. Dad was hopeful we would catch dinner on the way to the campsite. So far, no such luck. While we were waiting I asked Mom if I could go to the stream and fish. After being granted permission, I baited my fishing pole and headed down the bank. I was so proud to be holding my own fishing pole. I was hopeful of catching a fish and making Daddy proud!

I had been at the stream about ten minutes when I suddenly felt something pull on my line! Truly! Could it be a fish? I was so excited. I started yelling, "I caught something! Something is on my line!" My mother and sister came running. They were as excited as I was. Mom started instructing me. "Reel in your line slowly, carefully. Take your time."

Then—there it was! My very first fish, on my new fishing pole! Joy of joys. I thought it looked like a good size, enough to feed the whole family! But here was the reality of it: it barely met minimum size to keep. Yet I was overjoyed.

One thing I hated about eating a fish dinner was the little bones I kept finding. I asked my mom to please clean it so there were no bones left in it. She smiled and said, "I tell you what, Derry Lee, this is your fish—your very first fish. I think you should clean and debone it yourself." Hmmm. I wasn't sure what to think of that. It seemed like a good idea, but not a pleasant task. Nevertheless I went at it with gusto. I was determined there would be no bones left in my fish. After Mom

160

fried up my "little" trout, I realized I had also left very little meat under the skin.

When my parents determined that since it was my first fish, and since I had cleaned it soooo well, I didn't have to share it, I was both thankful and disappointed. Mom breaded it and fried it up for me. I took my plate with pride, sat on the nearest rock, and ate my delectable meal with a heart over-flowing with gratitude and excitement.

Intervention Kiss:

Jesus ate fish with His disciples. He showed them where to fish so they could fill their nets. Jesus saw the heart of a little girl and blessed her with a fish that afternoon.

Nature encounter "kiss" number two:

In that day I will make a covenant for them With the beasts of the field, With the birds of the air, And with the creeping things of the ground. ...To make them lie down safely.—Hosea 2:18.

My husband and I loved nature. We raised our children to love nature as well. We enjoyed camping and backpacking. Often we would sit quietly and study birds and animals that ventured near us. Creatures of the wild were interesting and entertaining. Watching and studying their habits taught us more about God and His love and offered character-building lessons.

Because of our love of being out in nature, we choose a parcel of land on 40 acres in the country to build our home. While we were building our home we lived in the garage. We had it partitioned off nicely. Across the side we had the boys' bedroom area. Along the other side where the shop was going to be was the master bedroom. In the center front was the living room area and behind that was the kitchen. The kitchen had a small "shop" sink in a counter. In the very center of the garage, between the end of the kitchen area and the beginning of the living room area was our wood stove. Being central, it provided heat for the whole garage. The room was cozy and inviting.

One cool fall night shortly after the children had fallen asleep, my husband came in with a parcel in his arms wrapped in a towel. I couldn't imagine what he had, but I would soon find out. He was so excited! He had captured a skunk! "I think he's cold," my husband announced.

While I love wildlife, I admit I wasn't excited about having a skunk wandering around our very small habitat. I was more than concerned as he sat the skunk down and turned it loose. What if when the children woke up they frightened our little friend in their excitement? What if he decided he needed to protect himself against us, then what? What if we made a move too quickly near our new friend and panicked him?

Nevertheless my husband permitted our "friend" to wander the premises. By the afternoon of the second day it was agreed the risks were too great. We were excited about our new pet and unsettled at the same time. He quickly received his freedom.

All was well until two nights later. We received another surprise package. On the way home my husband and our son Brian had found another critter roaming the streets late at night. This time the removal of the towel revealed an opossum! Brian was thrilled. He had helped catch it. He was already thinking of the right name for it.

It was obvious to me that this guy needed a cage. We happen to have an animal carrying cage nearby so for the night that would have to be his new home. Have you ever been close enough to an opossum to notice how terrible they smell?

162

Let me tell you, they have a horrible odor! This little guy lived with us for several weeks but had to be moved out of the garage "apartment" into the house construction area because his odor was so bad.

Even with the risks ... and foul fragrance ... there is a certain thrill in being close to animals that are not usually considered pets—animals that you only see in the wild. The presence of these two critters, even for a short time, somehow drew us closer to the Creator and enhanced our desire to study more of God's creation.

We loved reading Eric Hare's adventures with animals. His stories definitely sparked our enthusiasm to be bolder in our encounters with anything moving and breathing!

Intervention Kiss:

The joy of being so close to animals that we aren't normally able to interact with brought appreciation, compassion and deeper respect for God's creatures

Nature "kiss" number three:

A righteous man has regard for the life of his beast, ...
—Proverbs 12:10 RSV.

One of my minister friends called late one afternoon and asked if she could walk her dog on my property. I assured her she was welcome.

Soon after she arrived I heard loud excited barking out behind my home. A few minutes later my friend was at the front door reporting excitedly that her dog had cornered a deer under my pool deck. When the deer tried to escape it banged into the deck. She was concerned that in its fright it had injured itself because it had fallen and was not moving. I suggested we give it a few minutes then go out and check on it. Maybe it was just stunned.

About 15 minutes later we went out to check on the deer. It was still down. I approached it slowly so as not to frighten it further. It could not get up. It began snorting at me. I started singing "Jesus Loves You" and it settled down. I backed off. I like to believe all of creation knows the name of Jesus. This isn't the first time I have done it with results.

Another 30 minutes or so went by. I checked it again. The deer lay there unmoving. I approached again. No movement. No sound. I started praying for it. I asked God to breath life into the deer and revive her. Still no response. I didn't want a dead deer left there all night to entice wild animals so I decided I better call the Sheriff's department and ask for help.

As a chaplain I worked with many of them and knew them well. I had heard they would also help with this kind of a problem. When I called they said they would be out in about 30 minutes. I asked that they knock at the door so I could show them where the deer was.

Thirty minutes, 40 minutes, an hour went by and no sheriff. I finally suggested that my girlfriend go ahead and go home and I would deal with the situation. An hour and a half went by. The sun had gone down and it was beginning to get dark. Knowing that more important issues could have caused a delay in them coming I decided to call the Sheriff's office again and find out when to expect them.

When I called the person on the phone said, "Oh, we were already out there and couldn't find a deer."

I responded, "I didn't know you had been here. I asked that you guys knock at the door so I could take you to the place where the deer is down. It is just outside my pool area."

"That's where we looked. There is no deer down."

"I was just out there about 30 minutes ago and it wasn't moving. Let me go out and check while I have you on the phone." I headed outside and lo and behold—no deer!

I came back to the phone and said, "Well surprise of surprises. I didn't hear you guys come and now I see that you're right. The deer is no longer there. I can't believe it. That little doe was so still. I was sure she was dead."

The voice on the other end of the line said, "Is this you Chaplain Derry? Did you pray for that deer?"

The response made me laugh. "Well yes. Actually, I did."

"Then why are you so surprised?" he said.

He was right. Why was I so surprised?

Intervention Kiss:

God loves His creatures and He cares that we love them too. That deer looked dead. I came up close to it and it didn't flinch and it didn't appear to be breathing. I believe God heard my prayer of intercession and breathed life into it.

Nature "kiss" number four:

For you shall have a covenant with the stones of the field, And the beasts of the field shall be at peace with you.—Job 5:23.

I lived out in the mountains in a small log cabin with my husband and two baby boys. One son was two and a half and the other was about one. It was winter. We had had the first snowfall. The cabin door was glass providing a view of the great outdoors. A crackling fire was in our woodstove. The house was warm and toasty.

It was about dusk. I saw movement outside some distance away and wondered what it was. I gazed out the door to see what was out there. Then I spotted it—a cat crouched down in the snow starring my direction. I opened the door and called to it. It stared. I went to the kitchen and poured a bowl of milk and set it outside the door and went back in, but the cat ran off.

The next morning I saw that the bowl of milk was empty. So, that evening I set out another bowl of milk. I did this several evenings in a row at exactly the same time—after the children were in bed so they wouldn't scare the cat off.

One evening the cat came while I was just inside the door. Gingerly it crept up, keeping a watchful eye on me. I sat down inside the door unmoving and speaking gently to the cat. On the alert, he lapped up the milk and dashed off. We went through several evenings of this. Then I put on my jacket and left the door open.

The cat still came keeping his eyes on me but allowing me to be there. I kept talking gently trying to soothe him. Then I dared to reach out to pet him. He dashed off. The next night he pulled away. The next night he tolerated me. The next night he let me pet him. Several more nights passed.

I began to lure him into the house by moving the bowl of milk and food closer to the warmth of the fireplace. Several nights of this passed. He finally seemed comfortable coming into the house. Sooo, I made a fatal mistake and closed the door.

This wild cat I thought I had tamed, who was allowing me to draw him into the house and sit next to him and pet him, suddenly went completely out of control and scared me to death. He screeched and howled and began racing through the house, jumping on the furniture, climbing up the curtains, running over the counters in the kitchen banging into the windows to get out. I was so frightened, I couldn't get the front door open fast enough. He had gone berserk!

The next evening I didn't know what to expect. I repeated my routine, except I left the door open and froze us out. To my surprise, the cat finished eating, snuggled into the cat bed I had placed by the fireplace, and went to sleep. I left the door open and we snuggled up under the blankets. I wasn't sure what to do. The next night the same thing happened only this time I sat next to the bed and stroked him. He started purring.

That was when the transition was made. He became a part of the family and started sleeping at the foot of our bed.

Intervention Kiss:

Thank You Father for Your gift of pets—chosen by You to add enjoyment to our lives. Thank You for the lessons of patience and perseverance I learned as I worked to gain this cat's trust. What a wonderful pet he became. Thank You for that gift. Help us remember some things are worth waiting for.

Nature "kiss" number five:

But now ask the beasts, and they will teach you; And the birds of the air, and they will tell you; Or speak to the earth, and it will teach you; And the fish of the sea will explain to you. Who among all these does not know That the hand of the LORD has done this,—Job 12:7-9.

Those of you who have put up hummingbird feeders are well aware of how aggressive hummingbirds can become. One day we had a very aggressive hummingbird show up on the scene. He decided he was going to take over the territory. Up until then all the other hummingbirds had gotten along quite well. Then he showed up. He had iridescent coloring. He was absolutely beautiful and he must have known it because he had an attitude. He was bigger than the others and a bully. We watched him poke at the other hummingbirds as they came to the feeder. We saw him try to frighten them away. He was making the feeder his own and he wasn't about to share it with any of the other birds.

One little guy decided to brave it. He was sipping the nectar when the aggressive hummingbird poked him then took hold of his little feet and pulled him down and buried him in the ivy right below the window.

We were so amazed at what we had just seen that it took us a minute to process it, but my son ran out the door and quickly looked through the ivy. He picked up a very stunned hummingbird. He held him gently on his palm until he revived, shook himself and took off. A few minutes later the little bird came back and tapped at our window, looking in, as if to say, "Thank you."

Intervention Kiss:

The ability to hold the hummingbird in hand and experience the gratitude shown by this little creation of God. What an example. Thank You, Jesus. May we not fail to be grateful.

And yet more Nature "kisses":

O LORD, how manifold are Your works! In wisdom You have made them all. The earth is full of Your possessions—Psalm 104:24.

The earth is full of His possessions, yes! So many fun and even brief experiences of witnessing nature cross our path.

 Nature Kiss: We got to watch a young alligator walk across the park in our backyard in Florida. He ambled along to the next pond as we stood quietly tracking his journey.

We occasionally had alligators visit our neighborhood pond and those who lived around the pond had come to take turns naming them. It was our turn. We named him "Riley" which means brave. We all learned an interesting lesson from Riley. When you get too familiar with "the dangerous" it suddenly doesn't seem so frightening or threatening. Just like sin, we can become too comfortable and forget the potential danger to our future. It never pays to compromise or take unnecessary risks.

Nature Kiss: While on vacation in Costa Rica on a riverboat cruise, a monkey leaned over from the tree on shore and grabbed my banana. He was greedy and selfish. Are we?

Nature Kiss: When we were out kayaking, the manatees swam next to us—so close we could reach out and touch their backs. Were they looking for a friend?

Nature Kiss: On a different kayaking trip we watched the beach come alive with sand crabs feeding. Community!

Nature Kiss: I had been praying I would see a moose when I was in Newfoundland visiting my son. I was on the way to the airport and had yet to see one. I started praying again and hooray, while we were driving a moose stepped out to meet the car and stuck his nose against the window, looked in and walked off. God's gift!

Nature Kiss: While we were enjoying the cool of the evening in Florida, we heard two owls screeching and carrying on in the tree outside our lanai. A reminder that quarreling publicly affects everyone around.

Nature Kiss: Let's end this section with the time we went horse-back-riding up in the mountains. When we got to the meadow, each step the horses took sent monarch

butterflies spreading their wings in flight all around us. The field was covered with butterflies. They landed on us and on our horses. They were everywhere. What a beautiful sight! It felt like we were in heaven. "Kisses from heaven" surrounded us—filling us with awe and ministering to our souls and spirits.

There are so many ways God sends us kisses through nature. These are special moments that bring us pleasure and remind us how all of creation belongs to Him. Romans1:20 *For since the creation of the world His invisible* attributes *are clearly seen, being understood by the things that are made,* even *His eternal power and Godhead, so that they are without excuse.*

Nature speaks to us if we will listen. Job 12:7-10 invites us, *"But now ask the beasts, and they will teach you; And the birds of the air, and they will tell you; Or speak to the earth, and it will teach you; And the fish of the sea will explain to you. Who among all these does not know That the hand of the* LORD *has done this, In whose hand is the life of every living thing, And the breath of all mankind?*

In the following verses we learn how all of nature will be praising God and honoring Him. Quite remarkable!!! Nature has much to offer us.

In Nehemiah 9:6, *You alone* are *the* LORD; *You have made heaven, The heaven of heavens, with all their host, The earth and everything on it, The seas and all that is in them, And You preserve them all. The host of heaven worships You.*

Romans 11:36, F*or of Him and through Him and to Him* are *all things, to whom* be *glory forever. Amen.*

Revelation 5:13, *And every creature which is in heaven and on the earth and under the earth and such as are in the sea, and all that are in them, I heard saying: "Blessing and honor and glory and power* Be *to Him who sits on the throne, And to the Lamb, forever and ever!"*

May we thank God for nature and thank Him as the Creator! The Creator of the universe Who cares for all His creation, is the same God Who is concerned about every *little* thing in our life, too.

Therefore submit to God. Resist the devil and he will flee from you.
—James 4:7

Laryngitis And Speaking Appointment

The phone rang. I answered ... but no words came out of my mouth. I had a bad case of laryngitis! The schedule had been set months in advance. I had been working on my presentations and handouts. I was up early because I needed to pack and get things in order before I left for the weekend. This was a couples retreat weekend. The presentations were about relationships—between couples and parents and children. The first meeting started that evening. I was the main presenter. It was too late to cancel. What was I going to do?

I called one of my prayer pals and whispered in the phone as loud as I could. She heard me. I explained my predicament and asked her to pray for me. We prayed and said goodbye. I went in to make some hot lemon water hoping that would help clear my throat and strengthen my voice.

A few minutes later my friend called back. She said, "I was praying for you and I believe God impressed me to encourage you to go to warfare against the enemy. Rebuke satan, in the name of Jesus and tell him to release your voice."

171

Thank you, Joyce! I immediately went to battle. I started quoting scripture, using the Word of God against the devil. When Jesus was up against satan he said, "It is written …." and then quoted scripture. That's what I started doing. I started out in a whisper. I persevered. The more I spoke out against satan, the stronger my voice became, until I was speaking clearly.

The enemy knew what I had to share over the weekend would be a threat to his destruction of families and he didn't want me there. John 10:10 says, *The thief* [devil] *does not come except to steal, and to kill, and to destroy. I have come that they may have life, and that they may have* it *more abundantly.*

Intervention Kisses:

God answered my prayer and let me keep my commitment for the seminar and witness couples' relationships revived and healed. When our plans seem to be interrupted—we need to talk to God. What is His plan?

There is power and authority in the name of Jesus. In James 4:7 we are told *Therefore submit to God. Resist the devil and he will flee from you.* God's Word is true. I submitted to God. I stood in the authority given to us against the power of the devil. I resisted and he had to release my voice at the victorious name of Jesus the Lord. Let us stand firm in Him and stomp the devil.

Let each of you look out not only for his own interests, but also for the interests of others. Let this mind be in you, which was also in Christ Jesus.
—Philippians 2:4-5

Pray at all times in the Spirit, with all prayer and supplication. To that end keep alert with all perseverance, making supplication for all the saints,
—Ephesians 6:18 RSV

Life Raft

Since I was in my early twenties, I have faithfully claimed the promises of God found in scripture. A number of years ago I was on a camping trip with my family. I awoke to a beautiful morning. I lay in my sleeping bag listening to the quiet breathing of my loved ones around me and the songs of birds worshipping God at the break of day. God seems especially close when you are closed in by His creation.

I began to worship God in my heart, praising and thanking Him. After some time, I desired to add Bible reading and promise claiming to my time of devotion and meditation. When I claim promises from scripture, I turn the pages of the Bible frequently. Turning pages in a silent environment can suddenly sound very loud as the paper crackles. I feared I would wake up my family.

If they woke up, excitement about the day would cause chatter to ensue. This sacred time with God would be interrupted. I decided that the best plan would be to review Bible promises that I could remember and begin claiming them in my mind.

After about 10 minutes of this, for the first time ever, I began to question what I was doing. I said, "Father do I have myself in some kind of habit that has become rote and routine? Am I honoring You or disappointing You by doing this promise claiming, some of the same ones, day after day? Is this really what You want me to be doing? I know there are some denominations that have all their prayers written out and they faithfully read and pray them every day, repetitiously. Have I gotten locked into something that displeases you?"

I laid there waiting for an answer. God answered me by giving me a picture. In my mind's eye I visualized myself in the middle of a large body of water—a lake or an ocean. I was holding onto a life raft with each hand. They were filled with people. I was hanging onto the one in front of me and I had my other hand on the one behind me. Then for just a moment, I released my grip on the life raft behind me. That was all it took. It slipped away. I could not retrieve it. It drifted further and further behind until it was no longer in view. In one moment I lost them! I got tired and stopped holding on and could not retrieve them.

The Lord in 1 Timothy 2:1 admonishes us, *Therefore I exhort first of all that supplications, prayers, intercessions,* and *giving of thanks be made for all men,* What happened to all those people I was holding onto? It was in that quick picture, I sensed the Lord saying, "I need you to intercede for my people because they don't do it for themselves. Without intercession, they may be lost forever. Don't stop. Don't stop. These promises are for you and for those I give you. Be faithful."

Many people have been lost who might have been saved if others had not given up or become distracted or overwhelmed with the responsibility of intercession. Sometimes just a helping hand or a word of encouragement can be enough to exemplify our Savior's love and character. Hebrews 7:25 RSV says, *Consequently he is able for all time to save those who draw near to God through him, since he always lives to make intercession for them.*

174

I will reach people you will never meet, and you will reach people I will never meet; people whom God has given you. The way we reflect Christ to others, and our faithfulness in interceding for them, may make the difference in their eternal salvation. And we are not alone in this, Romans 8:26 RSV assures us, *Likewise the Spirit helps us in our weakness; for we do not know how to pray as we ought, but the Spirit himself intercedes for us with sighs too deep for words.* The angels stand with us to reach God's children.

Intervention Kiss:

The importance of intercession, applying the power of His word is a calling of God which also rejuvenates faithfulness in prayer.

 Butterfly Kiss:
We are like butterflies who flutter for a day and think it is forever.
—Carl Sagan

Sow your seeds in the good ground, and they will prosper and bring forth fruits for you, both spiritual and material.

—Author unknown.

Every good gift and every perfect gift is from above, and comes down from the Father of lights, with whom there is no variation or shadow of turning.—James 1:17.

"It shall come to pass That before they call, I will answer; And while they are still speaking, I will hear.
—Isaiah 65:24

Memorial Service Assignment

The hospital was full. It had been a busy morning making patient rounds. There were many left to see. It was time to take a break, unwind and get centered.

I had just returned to the office when the phone rang. The person on the other end of the line told me the local funeral home had suggested they call me. They had no one to do the memorial service for their loved one the next day. They hoped I could do it. I was hesitant. Due to my high patient load and difficult cases, I really didn't want to do the service and suggested they contact someone else. Every suggestion I made, they countered. They were out of options, so I agreed.

It was a long summer day. That would give me time to stop by the house after work before I met with them to discuss the details of the service.

As I drove up the driveway, I again noticed the tile on my roof. Some of them were chipped, some loose, some had fallen off. My roof was badly in need of repair, and so were my finances.

When God had directed me to buy it from my husband, I had given the house back to God. I would be steward of it and He could fill it with whomever He chose. As steward however, I consulted Him. Now I needed to talk to Him about the roof situation and the fact that I thought it needed more repair than I had saved up in the house maintenance account. I also didn't know whom to call. All this I presented to Him for assistance as I drove up the driveway.

That evening, I met with the family and went over the plans for the next day. They decided they just wanted a graveside service.

The next day I arrived at the cemetery a bit early. People were beginning to arrive behind me. Only a few people were present. I introduced myself and offered words of sympathy and support. As I was visiting, a middle-aged man approached me. He introduced himself as a brother to the wife of the woman who had lost her husband. He thanked me profusely for all of my help and for my willingness to be there. He then began sharing about the family and about himself. In the midst of the conversation he mentioned that he was a roofer. I couldn't help but look at him in disbelief. I asked if he worked locally. He responded in the affirmative.

I told him he had a talent I might have need of and asked for contact information. Surprised, he said, "Call me. I'll come over sometime next week and take a look at what you need. After all you have done for my sister, I promise you I'll give you a good deal."

And he did! God intervenes again. God orchestrated my doing a service for someone who needed me and in turn gave me someone I needed. What a fun, fun God. I called out to Him and He provided. He already had things lined up before I asked and revealed who I needed to get the job done. Thank You again, my Father. God knows who you need, too.

Intervention Kiss:

God orchestrated my schedule with those who needed my gifts and talents with those who could bless me with theirs, and my roof was repaired at a discounted price within my budget.

Trust in the Lord with all your heart, And lean not on your own understanding;—Proverbs 3:5.

 Butterfly Kiss:

Beautiful and graceful, varied and enchanting, small but approachable, butterflies lead you to the sunny side of life. And everyone deserves a little sunshine.

—Jeffrey Glassberg

 Butterfly Kiss:

A child is like a butterfly in the wind. Some can fly higher than others, but each one flies the best it can. Why compare one against the other? Each one is different. Each one is special. Each one is beautiful.

—The Learning Station

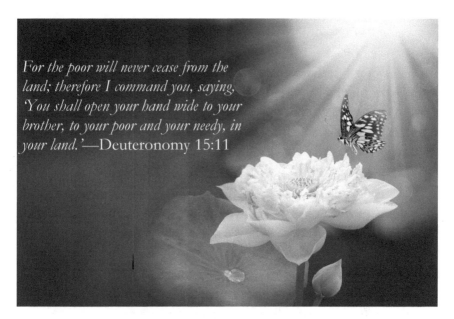

For the poor will never cease from the land; therefore I command you, saying, 'You shall open your hand wide to your brother, to your poor and your needy, in your land.'—Deuteronomy 15:11

Rescue Repercussions

I was a busy homeschooling mom, presently with four of our sons in the program. We devoted one day a week to other community homeschoolers. Our school sponsored an "Opportunity Plus Day." That was the day parents took turns teaching their line of expertise to children other than their own. It was also the day we had band and choir together.

It had been a long day. Our group had just been dismissed and I was assessing the supplies for supper when the phone rang. It was our pastor. He said, "I need your help. Will you look into something for me?"

"What's up?" I questioned.

"I just received a call that a family of seven children has apparently been abandoned. They have no father living at home and their mother has been gone three days with no word. The older children ages 14 and 15 have been looking after the other children. There are babies in the family too. Can you see what's going on over there?"

"Sure," I agreed. "I will head over there within the hour."

When I arrived the children were excited to have company. The older children looked worn out. They were beginning to prepare pancakes for supper. They were perplexed because they only had enough flour for a few pancakes, not enough to feed all of them. They were also feeding them to their dog because there was no dog food left.

I quizzed the girls about their mom. She had taken off with a man a few days previously and they hadn't heard from her. They were worried. They were out of food and out of diapers for the baby. The children looked like they had been playing outside and hadn't had a bath in some time.

I told them I had a good idea! Why don't you feed your dog the pancakes and all of you pack an overnight bag. You can come stay with us. We'll think of something fun to have for dinner tonight. That brought a joyful response of agreement.

As they were getting their things together I was trying to figure out what I would do with all of them, if I had enough clean towels and what we would have for dinner. We fed the dog, cleaned up the kitchen and watered the plants.

We loaded everybody in the car and were headed back to our house when God spoke directly to me with a warning. Heeding His advice I stopped at the drug store, loaded the basket with diapers and armed myself with several bottles of de-licing shampoo. The thought of that problem had not occurred to me. I had never dealt with lice before and didn't know what I was in for.

As soon as we got home I instructed the children to head upstairs to the bathroom. I asked the older children to bath and shampoo the younger ones while I prepared supper. They were so grateful. The older girls thanked me over and over. They were familiar with this process and knew it was needed. They were well-versed on how to use lice combs to scan for lice. It was all new to me. I watched and assisted.

After reading about lice I realized I had just contaminated my whole house. It was too late! The next day after some good food in their tummies, they spent a lot of time outside in the fresh air doing their schoolwork and getting some exercise.

I had previously called the pastor and told him I had the children and had left a note at the children's house for their mother. He was in complete agreement with what I had done. In the note I had given her my phone number and address reassuring her that I had all her children and they were fine.

We had finished supper and were ready to transition to the next activity when a car pulled into the driveway. Mom and her boyfriend had just arrived. She was a bit reserved but expressed her gratitude for me helping her children.

A month later, I was served a subpoena. Social Services wanted to place the children.

I was called to share how I had become involved and what I had done with the children. I was able to share that the pastor had called me because I homeschooled and would be able to put the children into class activities.

It was very interesting, even a bit disconcerting. Once I mentioned homeschool the questioning went from focusing on the children and home conditions to my homeschool and my qualifications, program, and assessment of my own children.

As I sat on the witness stand, I began to claim God's promise in Matthew 10:16-20, *"Behold, I send you out as sheep in the midst of wolves. Therefore be wise as serpents and harmless as doves. But beware of men, for they will deliver you up to councils and scourge you in their synagogues. You will be brought before governors and kings for My sake, as a testimony to them and to the Gentiles. But when they deliver you up, do not worry about how or what you should speak. For it will be given to you in that hour what you should speak; for it is not you who speak, but the Spirit of your Father who speaks in you.*

God kept his word. He was present with me. The Holy Spirit took over. Wisdom beyond myself poured forth from my mouth as promised in Luke 12:12, *For the Holy Spirit will teach you in that very hour what you ought to say.* In my heart I kept praying the promise in Luke 21:15, *for I will give you a mouth and wisdom which all your adversaries will not be able to contradict or resist.*

The officials were very impressed with our school. What a relief. Every homeschooling parent knows they can be under investigation at a moment's notice. We had unexpectedly been cleared in court under the judge's approval. We were now out of their scrutiny.

Intervention Kisses:

Who would have guessed that this rescue mission would have so many repercussions? Not only the lice which God cleared from our home—no infestation, but also a court appearance that brought approval and favor for our school with important and prominent officials. Sometimes when things look like they are going wrong, God has a blessing hidden within. Trust Him and hold fast.

But do not forget to do good and to share, for with such sacrifices God is well pleased.—Hebrews 13:16.

The LORD shall preserve your going out and your coming in From this time forth, and even forevermore.
—Psalm 121:8

He guards all his bones; Not one of them is broken.—Psalm 34:20

Runaway Truck

When you are busy working outside and it's all hands on deck, no matter how hard you try it is almost impossible to keep your eyes on seven sons. One will invariably slip momentarily out of sight.

We had driven the truck down the hill filled with top soil. We shoveled it out on the flat and began to rake it down. While my guys were finishing that up, I headed across the drive to check the well's pump house. Within a split second our little Nathan had climbed back into the cab of the truck.

No one knows for sure what happened—but we know what we saw. Suddenly the truck started rolling down the very steep hill with our younger son in it, picking up momentum rapidly. I didn't see it happen, but God our Protector did and intervened as promised in Psalm 34:15, *The eyes of the LORD are on the righteous, And His ears are open to their cry,* by alerting his brother who saw him and ran for the truck. With heroic action, his older brother was able to jump in the truck and bring it to a stop. It was nothing short of a miracle. It is incomprehensible how he was able to run fast enough and even open the door of the runaway truck to get inside and put the brakes on, but by God's grace he did!

Intervention Kisses:

I know the angels were watching over both of them, protecting their lives and keeping them from harm. Thank You again Father for Your divine intervention and sending angels to guard and protect my family. Thank You that You have a plan and destiny for each person. Help us to be willing to allow you to fulfill that plan in us, assured that Your eye is on us—to protect and keep us.

You did not choose Me, but I chose you and appointed you that you should go and bear fruit, and that your fruit should remain, that whatever you ask the Father in My name He may give you.
—John 15:16.

these are the things God has revealed to us by his Spirit. The Spirit searches all things, even the deep things of God.
—1 Corinthians 2:10 NIV

Secret Revealed

When my sons were living at home, growing up, I would ask God to be the revealer of secrets. I also petitioned the Lord to help my children get caught when they were guilty of doing wrong. God wants our children to spend eternity with Him even more than we do. He answered that prayer. God knew I could only be in one place at a time. He also knew what was happening when the boys were away from me and behind closed doors. He wants His children to have a pure heart and live righteously. Proverbs 4:23 NIV, *Above all else, guard your heart, for everything you do flows from it.*

As a mom, I could be a bit over protective, but I felt like that was my God-given responsibility. I'm accountable to God for how I raise my children and for the influences allowed in their lives. When I could not be there, I would count on God to reveal those things I needed to know.

I had a couple of older boys upset because the Lord would tell me when they were doing wrong and I would confront them. I would either confront them directly or I would confront the issue during family worship indirectly without singling anyone out. Most of the time, I wouldn't have to say anything.

The boys would come to me and say, "Mom, How did you know?"

I'd just smile and say, "Well, God has ways of letting me know because He loves you."

I had to be careful how this was shared because I wanted my sons to know God isn't their enemy, He's their friend. Their heavenly Father has their best in mind. It needed to be done in the right spirit. It's also intriguing how different personalities reacted.

I had one young man who got himself involved in some things he really wished he hadn't. He was embarrassed and didn't know how to talk to us about it, which was unusual. He talked about everything. Because I know him, I knew things weren't quite right and I had an uneasy feeling in my heart. I got on my knees and shared my heart with God. "Father, I feel in my heart that You're telling me I need to pray for a searchlight to go through this house and expose whatever's wrong. So, I pray that You'll reveal secrets to me."

Right up to that son's room, right to the place, right to his father, right to the phone, right to the school. He came home. He said, "Nobody had to tell me anything when you called for me to come, I knew what it was. I'm so glad you know. I've wanted to talk to you and I haven't had any idea how to tell you." He knew God's promise in Psalm 51:10 KJV to *Create in me a clean heart, O God; and renew a right spirit within me.*

Praise God for a God that cares about how we live our lives. Praise God for a God that will be the revealer of all secrets. Praise God for His unconditional love, forgiveness and for His desire to have all of His children spend eternity with Him.

188

Flee also youthful lusts; but pursue righteousness, faith, love, peace with those who call on the Lord out of a pure heart.—2 Timothy 2:22.

Intervention Kiss:

The cry of my son's heart precipitated God's love and exposure of my son's need to repent and walk in the freedom of "new beginnings." Every day can be a day of new beginnings. God is always waiting with arms open wide—no matter how wrong we have been, no matter what others think, He is there to help us pick up the pieces and start over.

Thus says the LORD, "Stand by the ways and see and ask for the ancient paths, Where the good way is, and walk in it; And you will find rest for your souls. But they said, 'We will not walk in it.' Jeremiah 6:16 NASB is a promise for us.

 Butterfly Kiss:

When you find yourself cocooned in isolation and you cannot find your way out of darkness … Remember, this is similar to the place where caterpillars go to grow their wings.

—Necole Stephens

Oh, give thanks to the LORD, *for* He is *good! For His mercy* endures *forever.*—Psalm 107:1.

The human spirit was not created for bondage or fear ... Jesus brings His commanding presence to every situation if you ask Him.

—Author unknown. 1992 Prayer Journal, Peace.

Shocking Discovery

We had been living in the garage while we were building the house. Once we moved into the house, we left the old refrigerator in the garage but moved its placement.

It was handy to have it. It kept us from going to the market every other day. We ate a lot of nuts, grains and fresh food which needed to be refrigerated. With seven growing sons who ate like they were two people each, there was not enough storage in one refrigerator.

I was busy in the kitchen making dinner. The boys were all in the kitchen helping out as usual. I sent the two younger children to the garage refrigerator to bring in some vegetables for our meal.

A few minutes later they came back in tears. "We tried to get what you asked Mom but the refrigerator was shocking us. It was so bad it knocked me backwards."

"What are you saying? The refrigerator shocked you? How can that be?

I went out and gingerly put my hand on the handle. I got a bad shock. I had just gotten something out of the frig a few minutes before and had no problem. What was going on?

It turned out that when the pump for the well went on it somehow caused an electrical short in the other line ... or something. The cause was discovered by observing a line of earthworms that were surfacing along the path of the electrical line to the well. They too were getting shocked and were trying to escape. The wire hadn't been grounded properly and consequently the boys' shocking discovery led to an important repair.

What might you need to address that has been hiding in the background waiting to "bite" you? Ask God to reveal it to you today.

Intervention Kisses:

Thank You Father for sending Your angels to guard our children. Shocking ground became holy ground by heavenly presence. You cleared up the mystery and protected us from a more severe consequence by revealing a serious problem that needed to be addressed.

 Butterfly Kiss:

May the wings of the butterfly kiss the sun

And find your shoulder to light on.

To bring you luck, happiness and riches.

Today, tomorrow and beyond.

—Traditional Irish Blessing.

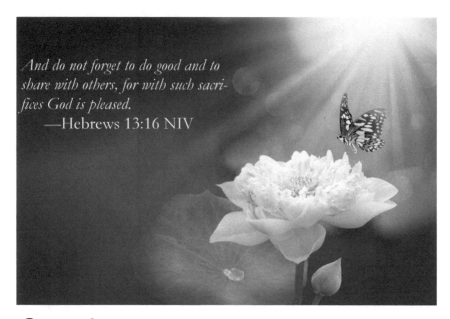

And do not forget to do good and to share with others, for with such sacrifices God is pleased.
—Hebrews 13:16 NIV

Surprise

Have you ever heard or sung the song, "What a Friend I Have in Jesus"? Jesus is the kind of Friend you want to have on your team. He is faithful, loyal, protective, dependable, confidential, has wise counsel, is quick to forgive, always there for you, giving and sharing according to the needs of those around Him, and loves with unselfish and unconditional love.

My dear friend Karen in California demonstrates many of Jesus' qualities. I am blessed to have her in my life. I met Karen when she became a chaplain volunteer. I was not only blessed by her gift of ministry, but the department profited from her creative talents and technical skills.

She has become a friend who "sticks closer than a brother." Most importantly, besides being there for me when I moved or when I needed a friend to 'bounce things off of,' she is an amazing and dependable prayer warrior.

One day she blessed me with some self-created note cards made from photographs she had taken of a variety of beautiful flowers. Her cards are so exceptional, the pictures so exquisite, that I treasure them and am very selective as to how they are used. I have been out of them for a while. Since they were given to me as a gift, and since she will not allow me to purchase them from her, I had simply done without. However a longing in my heart for more cards had remained.

I had been away for several weeks and just returned home. The next day was my birthday. I received a number of cards and surprises in the mail. Among them was a package from Karen gifting me her beautiful and much-cherished cards.

As soon as I opened her package, I couldn't help but think of the scripture *A generous person will prosper; whoever refreshes others will be refreshed.*—Proverbs 11:25 NIV.

Because Jesus knows my every thought and desire, I considered her gift also a birthday gift from Him. Thank you both! Now because of the blessing I received, I could bless others too with cards that accentuate the beauty of nature, exposing God's creativity.

… Freely you have received; freely give.—Matthew 10:8 NIV.

Intervention Kiss:

God knew the desire of my heart was to bless other friends with the gift of Karen's talent, to share His creative beauty, and He placed it in her heart to gift me again with the cards she designs. He also knew, when He brought her into my life, I would cherish the gift of Karen herself and her friendship.

Thank You Lord for caring for our hearts' desires as well as our needs—no matter how small and seemingly insignificant they may be.

194

Be anxious for nothing, but in everything by prayer and supplication, with thanksgiving, let your requests be made known to God;—Philippians 4:6

Time For A Perm

We all have issues. One issue I struggle with is my hair. God gave me a lovely head of hair. It is sooo thick, I have to thin it in order to style it. When I was younger, I had an interesting problem with my hair … unexplainable. When I'd get nervous, my hair would go straight. You could actually watch my hair go straight in front of your eyes. Thankfully, I seemed to have grown out of that. But speaking of straight, it is straight as a board, so routinely I would get a perm just so I could do something with it. A straight hairstyle is not particularly becoming on me.

It was time again. I was way past getting a permanent. I had been on such a horrendous schedule I hadn't had the time. I had resorted to using hairspray and my curling iron hoping it would last an hour. I had a speaking appointment coming up and also my son's wedding. A lot to get ready for. I certainly didn't want to worry about my hair. I thought, 'When and where am I going to get a perm?' Usually my friends and I traded off giving each other perms. They were out of town so I was stuck.

With Kisses From Heaven

As is my habit, I called out to my Father in heaven for direction. It is always amusing when God immediately responds. The unexpected often occurs. And that's just what happened!

I was in town. My mission was to find some cushions for our patio furniture. We expected guests in for our son's wedding reception. I pulled into a place where I don't normally shop. There were no places to park right in front of it. I ended up a block down the street. When I got out of the car I noticed I had parked directly in front of 'Hair Depot'. The Lord invited, "Go in."

Now there were beauty parlors all over the town I lived in. This one was in a neighboring town about 20 minutes away. I had just prayed, asking for God's direction and here I was parked outside a beauty parlor. I thought, 'Okay, Lord.' I walked right in.

I walked up to the desk and introduced myself. "I'm badly in need of a perm, but I need to let you know that I am a real problem. My hair is perfectly straight. My friends and I give each other perms and we have done it for so long that we know exactly how it needs to be rolled so that it comes out right. I use two papers or my hair frizzes. If you don't want to deal with someone that fussy, it's okay. Just tell me, I'll go somewhere else. Besides, the rest of the story is I can't sit very long. I get antsy so I need someone who's pretty fast."

The gal stood there and started laughing, "I think we have three choices for you. But perhaps you should see the owner for her suggestions." The owner came out and recommended one beautician who she felt was worth waiting for.

"That's fine," I responded. I didn't realize that meant I had to wait two weeks. I didn't know if I could do that, my hair was so unruly. I did though, because I knew God had led me there in answer to my prayer and I knew He had chosen this particular beautician for me.

When the day finally came, since I was so convinced that the Lord had given me this woman, I wasn't really worried about my perm. I didn't spend much time praying about it like I usually do. I simply said, "Father, please help my perm to come out all right."

Everything was so hurried that morning, I only got halfway through my scheduled time of worship with the Lord, which always distresses me. But off I went.

The beautician the Lord had given me happened to be a Christian. She loved Jesus. When she found out I was a chaplain and I loved Jesus, after she washed my hair, she whispered in my ear, "Did you pray about this perm?"

So I told her what I have already shared with you. She grinned and said, "Well I prayed about it."

We talked about how we both had morning devotions. She asked, "Do you read a chapter in Proverbs, one day for each day of the month?"

Surprised by her question, I affirmed, "I do, do that.

"I also read a Psalm for whatever the date is and then add 30, and 30 again, until I'm to the end of Psalms.' she reported.

"I do that too." I said.

"Did you get to do your reading today?" she asked.

"No. I had to cut my time short to get here."

"Well, let me tell you what was in Proverbs 19 today." This is what she disclosed, "In that chapter of Proverbs verse 11, the Lord teaches us that if somebody wrongs you, you should ignore it." *A person's wisdom yields patience; it is to one's glory to overlook an offense.*—Proverbs 19:11 NIV. "You're not supposed to avenge yourself. Wait for the Lord to take care of it because He has a plan. Forgive them."

What she said reminded me of two other verses in Proverbs. Proverbs 20:22 NIV, *Do not say, "I'll pay you back for this wrong!" Wait for the LORD, and he will avenge you.* And also

197

With Kisses From Heaven

Proverbs 17:9 NIV, *Whoever would foster love covers over an offense, but whoever repeats the matter separates close friends.*

On and on she went. When she was all finished she said, "You know, isn't that funny? There were so many other things in that chapter. I don't know why I picked that out to share with you. I don't think I have anybody upset with me right now. As a matter of fact, I don't even think my family is upset with me. Isn't it funny that I would say that to you?" Standing there giving a perm she shared Jesus. She shared God's counsel. She lived her faith and witnessed to me.

I said, "No it's not funny. As a matter of fact, I'm going through a little situation and I was just to the point where I was going to make a visit and say, "Okay, you guys! This is how it really happened." I was ready to clear myself, but God has used you this morning to say, 'Zip it up, Derry. Just be quiet. Just keep loving, keep accepting, keep giving and be quiet. Because I will clear your name.'"

Intervention Kisses:

We never know when God will use us to touch another's heart. We never know when we will be God's answer for someone else, or they will be an answer for us. In my case, it happened when it was time for a perm.

God chose a beautician who kept me from making a mistake and prematurely addressing an issue by witnessing to me. In that meeting God reassured me He was going to take care of everything.

I also got a lovely workable perm!

And we know that all things work together for good to those who love God, to those who are the called according to His *purpose.*
—Romans 8:28.

Why Are You Crying?

In my book *With Gladness Every Day.* I share how I first met God as my personal friend. I tell stories of when my husband had a concussion and we had no money coming in. I share how the Lord filled our cupboards and how He filled my wardrobe and provided clothes for my sons.

At that same time, we were on the verge of losing our new home that we had worked and saved so hard to buy. This was our first home and it was a new home. Who wants to part with their new home? But there we were, bills piling up around us. I had a terrible problem with worry in those days; the whole situation seemed overwhelming to me. I would cry for hours as I contemplated the future. I was a new Christian and I had not yet learned to surrender everything to God, and trust.

We had two little boys to care for. The future seemed so bleak, dark and uninviting. I didn't know all my worry, anxiety and fears would be lifted in an intense time of prayer. I later found His word says in Isaiah 41:10 *Fear not, for I am with you; Be not dismayed, for I am your God. I will strengthen you, Yes, I will help you, I will uphold you with My righteous right hand.'* And in 1 Peter 5:6-8 NIV, *Humble yourselves, therefore, under God's mighty hand, that he may lift you up in due time. Cast all your anxiety on him because he cares for you. Be alert and of sober mind. Your enemy the devil prowls around like a roaring lion looking for someone to devour.*

If I had only known to ask God to do "according to His will," it would have saved so many tears. I realized if God didn't do something to help us we could lose our home.

Foreclosure notices began coming. I was receiving continual calls from collection agencies. "When are you going to pay your electric bill? We're turning it off, you know." It was so close to happening I remember going to my mother's to wash my hair. I was afraid they would turn off the water on me when my hair was full of shampoo, right in the middle of me washing it. That's how bad it was.

We had now been in this state of foreclosure for nine months. Generally the bank tried to get you out of the house after six months for missed payments. But we were nine months into this and still just receiving warning notices. Needless to say, I am distraught, crying out to God, "Save us. God, do something. God; sell the house or help us win a contest. Do something to help us pay off the bills."

I realized things were becoming so desperate, we would soon be evicted, so I was looking for another place to live. Everywhere I looked, that we could even afford, was much worst than I had imagined. I thought, "How am I going to raise my boys in this environment?" I was worried. I was frightened.

I remember lying on my bed, crying off and on for weeks. One day I cried out to the Lord, "Father, I'm not getting up off of this bed until you put a smile on my face." God was persevering with me. And at that moment, after nine months of struggling with this, it was like a light bulb went off in my head. God was actually talking to me. "Derry, why are you crying?"

"Lord, you know why I'm crying."

"Derry, why are you crying? You don't even know the outcome yet. If things do not work out as you hope they will, then you deserve a good cry. But if everything works out well, look at all the time and energy you have wasted. Stop crying, watch and wait."

From that moment on, my perspective of life changed. The promise in Psalm 130:5 NIV was being fulfilled in my life. *I wait for the LORD, my whole being waits, and in his word I put my hope.* There's no need to borrow trouble from tomorrow. If it doesn't turn out the way I want it to, then cry if I must. But why bother until then? Only God knows the end of a story. Worry no longer had a hold of my life. Luke 22:42 became a reality in my life and my heart's desire. ... *Nevertheless not my will, but Yours, be done."*

We didn't lose our house. The Lord sold it, paid up all our bills and gave us enough money to start over. God even made it fun. He tipped us off that a buyer was on the way, and let us know how much the buyer was going to offer for the house. We were prepared even before the buyer got there. A neighbor of a neighbor of a neighbor tipped us off.

Moreover I will appoint a place for My people Israel, and will plant them, that they may dwell in a place of their own and move no more; nor shall the sons of wickedness oppress them anymore, as previously,
—2 Samuel 7:10.

Intervention Kisses:

Thank You God for healing me from worry, both then and for the future. Thank You for providing new beginnings for our family in a log cabin out in the country with the job of caretaking.

Jesus is the answer. Give God time. There is an appointed time. He always has the answer for every situation in our life. We need to claim the promises in the word of God now, more than ever before. He knows where we each need to be at the close of this world's history.

and he said: "LORD God of Israel, there is no God in heaven or on earth like You, who keep Your covenant and mercy with Your servants who walk before You with all their hearts.—2 Chronicles 6:14.

Someone once said, Prayer is the moment when heaven and earth kiss each other.

Epilogue

Now you know more about me than I know about you!

I hope you will go to the end of this book, follow the information and share about yourself and how this book has spoken to you.

My sharing answers to prayer and life experiences has been written not only to bring you hope and increase your understanding of God's love but also to glorify God, give honor to Jesus, and express appreciation to the Holy Spirit. With David in Psalm 40:9-10, I declare, *I have proclaimed the good news of righteousness In the great assembly; Indeed, I do not restrain my lips, O LORD, You Yourself know. I have not hidden Your righteousness within my heart; I have declared Your faithfulness and Your salvation; I have not concealed Your lovingkindness and Your truth From the great assembly.*

I believe strongly in accountability partnerships. When you have trusting relationships, it is easier to share truthfully, from the heart, without reservation. We learn from each other and sharing gives us an awareness of how we really feel or how we are actually responding to situations in life. If the mistakes I have made in my life will prevent you from having to go through similar consequences, it will have been worth my sharing with transparency.

If any story I recorded here will heighten your awareness of a loving God Who will walk by your side through any circumstance of your life or has encouraged you to accept Him as the Lord of your life, then that is reward enough for my time spent. I hope you will share any life changes you have incurred with me.

If you are interested in more of my inspirational stories, you will enjoy reading the companions to this book, *With Gladness Every Day* and *With Love Overflowing.*

Perhaps you haven't yet met Jesus and would like the assurance that He also knows **your** name. To develop that personal relationship and learn how to pray effectively, I encourage you to look into my books *Praying in the "Yes" of God* and *Growing in the "Yes" of God*.

If you are convinced you would like to have things different in your life and you want to seal that decision, coming in the next few pages is a sinner's prayer and Prayer of Commitment. I invite you to read "Meaning Of Commitment To God" and take this opportunity to secure your new or renewed commitment to God by reading through the prayers, prayerfully initialing each paragraph you agree with and then signing at the end.

May God bless you on your continued spiritual journey.

Looking forward to meeting in heaven,
Derry

Be A Butterfly

The butterfly emerges from its shelter to face the world with new-found confidence. A wonderful transformation took place inside the cocoon: a rebirth.

You have the opportunity to experience a renewal also. With the faith of the caterpillar, come into His presence and emerge a butterfly—a new creation, with new beginnings.

—Author unknown

Be Who God Created You To Be

Therefore, if anyone is in Christ, he is a new creation; old things have passed away; behold, all things have become new.—2 Corinthians 5:17.

Newness in Christ is the process of growing into the fullness He intended for you and equipped you for in this life.

Too many strive for happiness itself. But happiness is not something that comes from being sought directly. Like a butterfly, when pursued, it flits away—always darting beyond your reach. But if you'll quietly become involved in the work at hand, don't be surprised if that butterfly lights right next to you when you least expect it! Happiness is a by-product of living the life God designed you to live, and of doing the work He has designed especially for you to do.

You are a special person. Every personality trait, physical characteristic, and experience in life that has made you what you are today, has been designed by God to fit you for the special work He has for you to do!

You are a unique person. [...] Let Jesus' life be your example and let His spirit speak directly to you.

When you answer God's call and fulfill the mission that He has designed specifically for you to fulfill, I'll guarantee that happiness will find you!

—Excerpts from Kay Kuzma's notes from
the 1988 Christian Women's Retreat.
"Designing God's Woman," p29.

Meaning Of Commitment To God

This **Sinner's Prayer**, when prayed in faith, is met with the love and grace of God Who gives the free gift of eternal life to the one who prays. Eternal life is a life with God that begins right here on earth and continues with God in heaven for eternity. The moment you pray you will be born again by the Holy Spirit (John 3:1-21). You will be a new person with a new identity. This may sound too good to be true but I assure you, if anything, I am understating the life and adventures that you can look forward to as you begin your journey with the Lord Jesus Christ and your fellow Christ followers.

Before you pray let's look at what the Bible has to say. For those who have read my book and are not familiar with the Bible, you should know the Bible is also referred to as the Holy Scriptures and the Word of God. It is a record of the relationship of God with mankind. The Bible is not like any other book ever written in the history of mankind, for it reveals the love of the one true God, the Creator of the heavens and the earth and seas and all that is in them, for the world and His desire to have a special people who will know Him and love Him.

The problem is sin. What is sin? The New Testament word for *sin* originates from a Greek term used in archery meaning to "miss the mark," the bullseye. If we are honest we all miss doing what we know is right at times. After all, we are only human and we do the best we can. Unfortunately the best we can doesn't meet the standard of a holy and righteous God.

There is a way that seems *right to a man, But its end* is *the way of death.*—Proverbs 14:12.

Therefore you shall be perfect, just as your Father in heaven is perfect. —Matthew 5:48.

For the wages of sin is *death, but the gift of God* is *eternal life in Christ Jesus our Lord.*—Romans 6:23.

206

for all have sinned and fall short of the glory of God,—Romans 3:23.

God's standard is perfection and it is not possible for anyone to obtain perfection apart from Christ. The only perfect person is Jesus Christ the Son of God Who imparts his righteousness to us.

For God so loved the world that He gave His only begotten Son, that whoever believes in Him should not perish but have everlasting life.
   —John 3:16.

Jesus said to him, "I am the way, the truth, and the life. No one comes to the Father except through Me.—John 14:6.

Jesus took the punishment for our sins when He suffered and died on the cross. There is no other Lord or Savior.

But what does it say? "The word is near you, in your mouth and in your heart" (that is, the word of faith which we preach): that if you confess with your mouth the Lord Jesus and believe in your heart that God has raised Him from the dead, you will be saved. For with the heart one believes unto righteousness, and with the mouth confession is made unto salvation.—Romans 10:8-10.

Accepting Jesus does not mean things in your life will be without trial or tribulation; but when you face them, you will have the assurance God is by your side and will see you through.

Christians are meant to have the same vocation as their King, that of cross-bearers. It is this conscience of a high calling and of partnership with Jesus which brings gladness in tribulations.—Richard Wurmbrand

A Sinner's Prayer

Do you believe Jesus is the Son of God Who died for your sins? Do you believe God raised Him from the dead? If you do and you want to make that confession, pray this simple prayer:

Father God, I believe that Jesus Christ is Lord and Savior. I believe you sent your Son Jesus Who died for my sins. I believe that He was raised from the dead. I ask you to forgive my sins.

Lord Jesus I ask you to come into my heart and be my Lord and Savior. I thank you for hearing my prayer and for saving me and giving me eternal life.

Heavenly Father, I ask you to fill me with the Holy Spirit and empower me to live the life you have called me to.

In Jesus' Name, Amen.

Now that you have placed your trust in Jesus Christ, let me encourage you to read the Bible and let God work His Word into your heart. Remember, you are not the same person you once were. Until now the world and circumstances have defined you, but now you have been born again; you are a new creation handcrafted by God. This doesn't mean you are perfect. It means you have a new perspective because Christ abides in you.

I encourage you to let God lead you to a Bible-based church that will teach you Truth from the Word of God and prepare you to be baptized as one of God's followers (disciples).

Therefore, if anyone is in Christ, he is a new creation; old things have passed away; behold, all things have become new.—2 Corinthians 5:17.

Prayer Of Commitment

If you want to make a recommitment to God, pray this Prayer of Commitment:

Father God, Lord Jesus, Blessed Holy Spirit;

Thank You for Your unconditional and sacrificial love for me. I desire to live out Your divine plan intended specifically for me.

Thank You that Jesus died that I may live. I choose this day to ask for forgiveness of my sins and accept Jesus' sacrifice on the cross for me.

I want You as Lord of my life and to live a life of answered prayer, walking in Your will, empowered by Your Holy Spirit. I will serve You gladly with wholehearted appreciation for all You have given, all You have done, and all that You offer.

I commit to live my life to honor You, my Lord. By Your grace, I will follow Your example. Help me become familiar with scripture, presenting the promises for fulfillment as I work in partnership with You. With joy I will share with others what God does for me, with me, and in me. Use me to love and influence souls for the glory of the Kingdom.

On this, the _____ day of _____, 20___, I choose to surrender my life to You; to offer my heart for Your dwelling place, and to follow wherever You lead me.

Signature: _____

I Saw A Butterfly Today

I was strolling through the woods one day
 When something caught my eye
I saw a little brown cocoon
 Trying to birth a butterfly

I watched the effort of that butterfly
 As she struggled to be free
I was vain enough to think
 She might need some help from me.

I knew while in her prison house
 That she had longed to fly
And I knew she must be anxious
 To spread her wings and try.

I saw a tiny wing emerge
 As the struggle carried on,
And I thought my pretty butterfly
 Would surely soon be gone.

But it seemed to take forever
    Which was the Master's plan
But I was still vain enough
    To think she needed man.

So I took my little penknife
    And I split her prison shell
And she came forth a butterfly
    But down to earth she fell.

She lay there a tiny limped mass
    Could not unfold her wings
For they had not received the strength
    That a struggling effort brings.

She would have been so beautiful
    A floating in the sky
But because I made it easy
    She could never ever fly.

Sometimes in life the same is true
    And easy way seems best
And we would like to drift along
    Without that struggling test.

But if all our life is lived like this
    And it comes our time to die,
How sad to face a life unlived
    For we never learned to fly.

—Rev. Raymond Merrill "Dick" Coolidge

If nothing ever changed, there'd be no butterflies.

Author unknown

Titles by Dr. Derry James-Tannariello

For gift or bulk orders of these, or any of Derry's books, please visit our website:

FreedomInSurrender.net

Heaven Touches Earth—Handbook for Supporting Sick, Terminally Ill and Dying was *written to provide you with the skills and tools necessary to bring solace and comfort to the sick and suffering at home, in the hospital or hospice ministry.*

This concise "how-to handbook" is also a succinct resource of clear insight into hospital practices and protocols useful in training volunteers, parish visitors, pastors and chaplains and a helpful refresher guide for those who have studied hospital ministry.

Heaven Touches Earth Companion— Healing and Deliverance Scriptures and Prayers *is a take-along resource containing only the Healing and Deliverance Scriptures and Prayers chapter of the* Heaven Touches Earth *book. It is designed for those ministering in a supportive role (63 pages).*

Also available in eBook format at Amazon.com, or at

FreedomInSurrender.net

Living Volumes One and Two:
Praying in the "YES" of God

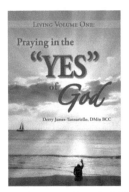

God knows your name! *Do you believe that? Do you believe there even is a God?*

Do you believe Jesus Christ knows who you are and is interested in your life? Do you believe He is Who He says He is, and can do what He says He can do?

When you pray, does it sometimes feel like your prayers are hitting the ceiling, or are falling on deaf ears? Are you angry with God because your prayers seem not to be answered? Have you given up asking God for things for yourself because you don't want to be disappointed again; or you're afraid if God is silent you will begin to question His existence, and then you'll have nothing to put your hope and trust in?

Praying in the "YES" of God *will help you find those answers and give you the tools to face the unknown with the peace and confidence that God loves you! Learn how to live with triumphant faith, peace of mind, and enthusiastic testimony.*

Growing in the "YES" of God

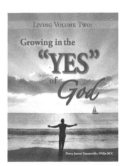

God Has a Plan for Your Life! *Do you wonder why it seems some people have answers to their prayers and unexplainable miracles in their life—and you don't? Is there really any such thing as security and joy? What does love mean? What if you could find the answers to these questions and more? You can.*

This in-depth Bible Study on principles of a more effective prayer life, further growth in Jesus and living out His character and plans for your life victoriously and blessed will reassure you of God's love. It is best understood and most effective if preceded by Living Volume One: Praying in the "YES" of God.

Also available in eBook format at Amazon.com, or at
FreedomInSurrender.net

Companion books:

With Gladness Every Day

Become confident in your walk with God and increase your trust and hope in Him. The stories in this book are answers to prayers and lessons from life experiences dependent on God's grace and mercy.

In this time of uncertainty and turmoil in our nation, are you mindful of the magnificence of God's love and the countless ways He expresses it to you each day? If not, it's time to reconnect to God's presence and awaken your senses to His unconditional, all encompassing love for you.

Be inspired by these stories, and let them arouse in you a desire to become acquainted with this King of kings, or renew your desire to commit all to Him and sing His praises!!!

With Kisses from Heaven

In these times of uncertainty God is attentive to you! What if those little interventions and unexpected surprises in your life were actually not coincidental ... they were acts of love? I have found they are not coincidental, but what I call "Kisses from Heaven"—divine interventions.

In this two-section book you will read true stories referenced to scriptures and discover how attentive God is to everything that concerns us through these accounts of His interventions. Whether you have a personal relationship with Him or not, you will see God was there for you, even when you were unaware of it. These stories are sure to remind you of God's interventions in your own life.

May your increased understanding of Him bring you security and hope when the trials of life attempt to overwhelm you.

Also available in eBook format at Amazon.com, or at

FreedomInSurrender.net

Upcoming Titles

With Love Overflowing

Love begets love and produces a heart of gratitude and adoration. The stories in this book confirm there is security in Jesus and peace during life's turmoil and storms. They tell of such an incomprehensible love that truly Jesus becomes irresistible when you know Him and realize that love.

In this world of chaos, we are looking for security, that place free from fear, a place where we know we are loved unconditionally and will be cared for no matter what. I found that place in the incomprehensible, overflowing love and protection of Jesus the Savior. May your heart be awakened to learn and understand more of Him and to experience Jesus for yourself.

Fill My Life, Lord

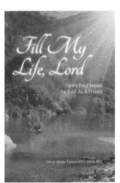

*What **fills** your mind, your heart, your home and your life depends upon what you allow to **fill** your hands.*

The stories in the Bible are not just stories to inspire and encourage you, but stories to build your relationship with God and change your life. What He has done in the past He will do for you in the present.

*If you don't have a personal relationship with God, I invite you to **fill** your hands with this book and open your mind and heart to this study. The Lord is waiting and willing to **fill** your life and prove He knows you and hears you. When you take one step towards the Savior, He runs the rest of the way to meet you. May your life be transformed.*

Why Not Bless Others!!!

FreedomInSurrender.net

- ✓ Mention this book on your social media platforms.

- ✓ Are you a blogger? Consider writing a book review on your blog. Post it to your blog and other retail book outlets.

- ✓ Know someone else who would be blessed by this book? Pick up a copy for a friend or coworker

- ✓ Recommend this book to your church library or small group study.

- ✓ Share this message on Facebook. "I was blessed by **With Kisses From Heaven** by Derry James-Tannariello and Freedom In Surrender Ministries."

Scan this QR code for
FreedomInSurrender.net